Andrew Jackson's Her

Mary French Caldwell

Alpha Editions

This edition published in 2024

ISBN : 9789366385716

Design and Setting By
Alpha Editions
www.alphaedis.com
Email - info@alphaedis.com

As per information held with us this book is in Public Domain. This book is a reproduction of an important historical work. Alpha Editions uses the best technology to reproduce historical work in the same manner it was first published to preserve its original nature. Any marks or number seen are left intentionally to preserve its true form.

Contents

FOREWORD: (1933) .... - 1 -
BOARD OF DIRECTORS OF THE LADIES' HERMITAGE
ASSOCIATION .... - 2 -
INTRODUCTION .... - 3 -
ANDREW JACKSON'S HERMITAGE .... - 7 -
ADDITIONAL NOTES .... - 76 -
FOOTNOTES .... - 83 -

FOREWORD: (1933)

By the late JOHN H. DEWITT, distinguished jurist and historian, who was President of the Tennessee Historical Society and Judge of the Court of Civil Appeals.

The history of the Hermitage, Andrew and Rachel Jackson, their domestic life, their relations with their friends and her kin, is of charming interest. Mrs. Mary French Caldwell has recorded in this booklet much of this history that has not hitherto been published. She has made patient research into old records and other documents, bringing to light Jackson's transactions in certain lands, his acquisitions of home sites, and building and rebuilding of homes. She has restated who were his immediate kin by affinity and his closest local friends. She has revived the color and atmosphere of life at the Hermitage in the years when its master was its beloved and dominating personality in the flesh.

The Ladies' Hermitage Association has done a fine service in publishing this manuscript for the benefit of all lovers of this history. It should be eagerly obtained and carefully studied by tourists as well as by all other Americans. They will profit by it in culture and in patriotism.

BOARD OF DIRECTORS OF THE LADIES' HERMITAGE ASSOCIATION

Mrs. Robert F. Jackson	*Regent*
Mrs. Wm. P. Cooper	*First Vice-Regent*
Miss Fermine Pride	*Second Vice-Regent*
Recording Secretary	*Miss Martha Lindsey*
Corresponding Secretary	*Mrs. Douglas Wright*
Treasurer	*Mrs. Roy Avery*

Directors: Mrs. George F. Blackie, Mrs. Charles E. Buntin, Mrs. Lyon Childress, Mrs. Paul DeWitt, Mrs. Edgar M. Foster, Mrs. E. W. Graham, Mrs. Douglas Henry, Mrs. Gilbert Merritt, Mrs. Jesse M. Overton, Mrs. William Weymss.

Board of Trustees: Mr. E. A. Lindsey, Nashville, Chairman; Mr. William E. Beard, Nashville; Mr. Henry Barker, Bristol; Mr. Lewis R. Donelson, Memphis; Mr. Lawrence Winn, Nashville; Mr. Herbert Gannaway, Memphis; Mr. Stanley F. Horn, Nashville; Dr. Marvin McTyiere Cullom, Nashville.

Regents of the Association have been: Mrs. Mary L. Baxter, Mrs. J. Berrien Lindsley, Mrs. Mary C. Dorris, Miss Louise Grundy Lindsley, Mrs. B. F. Wilson, Mrs. Bettie M. Donelson, Mrs. Harry Evans, Mrs. R. R. Henry, Mrs. Walter Stokes, Mrs. James S. Frazer, Mrs. Edward A. Lindsey, Mrs. Reau E. Folk.

Mrs. Jesse M. Overton, Mrs. E. W. Graham, Mrs. George F. Blackie, and the present regent, Mrs. Robert F. Jackson.

Publications Committee: Mrs. George F. Blackie, Miss Martha Lindsey and Miss Fermine Pride.

INTRODUCTION

It was not difficult to choose a name for this little volume. *Andrew Jackson's Hermitage* is neither new nor original, but it has had common usage for such a long period of years that it seems by far the most natural title for any work dealing with that historic old mansion which offered a haven of peace and contentment to "Old Hickory," during both the storms and the calms of his eventful career. In every respect it is Andrew Jackson's Hermitage. Its fertile fields sustained him, its trees sheltered him, and the friendly walls of the dwellings which he placed in the midst of its broad acres were not only his refuge in times of dissatisfaction with the outside world, but they formed the castle to which he welcomed his friends. It mattered little that the first Hermitage was an humble abode of logs. He was its master, and his guest, whether he happened to be the polished and elegant Aaron Burr or some uncouth backwoodsman, was given a royal welcome.

The mistress of the Hermitage—Rachel, the beloved and adored—was the *raison d'être* of the whole establishment. She was, to Andrew Jackson, the center of the universe—the one fixed thing around which all of the affairs of his life revolved. Her happiness was his greatest concern and, in building a home, her comfort and pleasure were his first consideration. She was not the kind of a woman, however, to accept such adoration without repaying it in thought and in deed. She was an excellent housekeeper, a gracious hostess, and an efficient manager of the whole plantation. Like many women of the South, she was often left for months at a time in charge of the entire estate, for travel was difficult and tedious, and men who participated in public affairs were forced to endure long absences from home. During the early years of their marriage General Jackson, either as an attorney or as judge, traveled hundreds and hundreds of miles over wilderness trails. His mercantile business, as well as his legal and political activities, took him frequently to Philadelphia, Natchez, or other distant points. Later, the Creek campaigns and activities leading up to the Battle of New Orleans kept him away from the Hermitage for months at a time. After the victory in 1815 Mrs. Jackson accompanied him on trips to Washington, to Florida, New Orleans, and other places where his fame drew great crowds around them. There never was a time, however, when fame had any attraction for Rachel. All that she asked was that the lord and master of the Hermitage be freed to return to their peaceful fireside.

Of General Jackson's devotion to his wife there are hundreds of evidences. From the time he killed Charles Dickinson in the duel provoked by a rash reference to the unfortunate circumstances of their marriage, until his dying day, he was known for his almost fanatical devotion to her, and his desire to punish anyone who might cast a slur upon her fair name. Only Rachel's suffering after Dickinson's death and her gentle restraint kept his fiery temper under control.

The Hermitage stands upon the spot which Rachel Jackson selected. The walls of its central portion sheltered her, and to-day they house many objects made sacred by her touch. In the long years which intervened between her death and that of her distinguished husband, her memory was kept green by his devotion. The young lovers who, during his last years, laughed and danced through the pleasant rooms and hallways of the old mansion and wandered in the moonlight to the magnolia-shaded tomb in the garden caught something of his immortal love story.

Both he and Rachel loved young people. They had no children, but in 1809 they adopted a baby—a nephew of Mrs. Jackson's—and down through the years the Hermitage was enlivened by the happy laughter of children and of young people: sons and daughters of neighbors, of Mrs. Jackson's kin, and of the General's friends and associates. There have been many brides and many happy wedding parties at the old mansion, and the General himself was not averse to lending a helping hand in cases where Dan Cupid did not make progress rapidly enough to suit him.

Nothing reveals the gentle, human side of Andrew Jackson more completely than a study of the contacts made through various avenues of his home life. Nor can anything else as thoroughly prove his wisdom and good common sense. He had the greatest deference for women and a great tenderness for children. He was a compassionate master of slaves, a great lover of horses and fine cattle, and an excellent farmer. He was a shrewd trader and a meticulous observer of his own debts to others—and theirs to him. His only bad business deals, and they were not many, were those where his affection for a kinsman or a friend got the better of his cold reasoning power.

The picture which it is hoped that this little volume will create in the minds of the readers is that of Andrew Jackson, the husband and father, the host to friends and neighbors, and to such of the nation's great as came to his doors; the farmer who delighted in the productivity of his broad acres; the merchant who rode each day to his store at Hunter's Hill or Clover Bottom; the warrior who returned with the laurels of New Orleans to a log house; the statesman, weary with fame and the long, lonely years, who came back to his Hermitage to sit out the remainder of his days near the tomb of his beloved Rachel.

It is this conception of Jackson that the Hermitage perpetuates. The little museum which was once the nursery of his grandchildren houses relics of his military career and a rare collection of his state papers. Of this side of his life the nation is already well informed. The house itself speaks eloquently of the life which once vibrated its now quiet rooms. His office is filled with books which knew the frequent touch of his hands; his dressing gown lies across a chair in his bedchamber, and the miniature of Rachel is in its accustomed place on the table at his bedside. In the parlors the portraits of his "military family" look down upon silent rooms which, when they knew them, were full of music and laughter. The dining room, once the center of a lavish hospitality, is quiet, and the kitchen is no longer filled with negroes, bustling about and singing before a great open fire. It requires no great powers of imagination to people these rooms again. The inanimate objects are there. They have been carefully preserved by a patriotic group of women who realized their value in time to keep them in their original setting. Down through the years they will be guarded jealously by women who follow in the footsteps of the founders of the Ladies' Hermitage Association, and so will be preserved the home of one of the greatest of all Americans and the setting of one of the most beautiful love stories of all times.

"The Hermitage—a thing we hold in trust,

As true men guard their forbears' swords from rust.

Forbid it, God, that there should ever come

In length and breadth of this fair land of mine,

Such dearth of patriots that a warrior's home

Should come to seem less holy than a shrine...."

(From "The Hermitage," Will Allen Dromgoole, *Nashville Banner*, Jan. 6, 1935.)

ANDREW JACKSON'S HERMITAGE

"Beginning at a Hickory tree...." There is something prophetic in the description of the tract of land which Andrew Jackson bought from Nathaniel Hays on August 23, 1804. Nothing had yet happened in the career of General Jackson which even hinted that his wiry strength of body and of will would some day win for him the enduring title, "Old Hickory." The long, weary, homeward march from Natchez with his loyal Tennesseans was a decade ahead of him. The battles of the Horseshoe and New Orleans and the fame which followed them were undreamed-of events of a shadowy, uncertain future. No one foretold that the hickory tree would become symbolic of the man, nor that the tract of land he was buying would some day be one of the nation's most important shrines. Certainly no one saw in the purchaser the future idol of the nation and the ruler of its destinies during a period which called not only for superior statesmanship, but for unconquerable will and determination.

It is even more interesting to trace the history of the Hermitage tract back to the original grant made by the State of North Carolina to Nathaniel Hays, on April 17, 1786, and to see that the hickory tree still holds the initial place in defining the boundary line. This old grant reads:

> "State of North Carolina. Know ye that we have granted unto Nathaniel Hays six hundred and forty acres of land in Davidson county including a spring which lies in the entrance into Jones' bent on the South Side of Cumberland River, *beginning at a hickory* and a hackberry in Colo John Donelson's line thirty-one poles South of his North East Corner, running thence along Samuel Hays line, East four hundred and eight poles to a white oak and mulberry, North two hundred and fifty one poles to a white oak corner to Hugh Hays line west four hundred and eight poles to a black walnut, South two hundred and fifty one poles to the Beginning. To Hold to the said Nathaniel Hays his heirs and assigns forever, dated the seventeenth day of April 1786.

"Rd. Caswell

"Daniel Smith Surveyor.

"J. Glasgow, Sec.

"James Buchanan Richd Jones."

The Jackson deed to this tract, dated August 23, 1804, showing a lapse of eighteen years from the original grant, describes the boundaries as follows: "*Beginning at a Hickory tree* and Hackberry on Colo John Donelsons line, now Savern Donelsons line, thirty-one poles South of his North East Corner Runing thence along Samuel Hays line, now his heirs, East two hundred and fifty four poles Crossing Spring Branch three poles to a Gum Taylors Corner Thence north with Taylors line Ten poles to a Small Hickory thence North nine Degrees East along Taylors line to a Black Oak Standing on the South Boundary line on Hugh Hays premption now belonging to the heirs of Samuel Donelson Des^d thence along Hugh Hays line West to a Black Walnut the South West Corner of Said Hugh Hays premption thence South two hundred and fifty one poles to the beginning it being a part of a Premption granted to the said Nathaniel Hays from the State of North Carolina by a patent bearing Date the Seventeenth day of April One Thousand Seven Hundred and Eighty six, and N^o twenty four to have and to hold the said Tract or Parcel of Land with its Appurtenances to the only use and behoof of the said Andrew Jackson his heirs and assigns forever and the said Nathaniel Hays doth by these presents Oblige himself his heirs Executors and Administrators to warrant and forever Defend the Right Title and Interest of the Said Tract or Parcel of Land with the Appurtenances thereunto Belonging to the said Andrew Jackson his heirs and assigns forever against the Claim or Claims of all and Every Person legally claiming the Same in Testimony whereof the said Nathaniel Hays has hereunto set his hand and affixed his seal the day and date first above and for than purpose mentioned.

"Nathl Hays.

"Witness John Coffee

"Vance Greer & Alex^r Donelson."

When this tract was finally deeded to the State of Tennessee in 1856, the description of boundaries had become more technical. The surveyor began his measurements at a stake in Kerr's line, and there is little in his description to remind the reader of the original boundary lines. The deed held by the State of Tennessee contains, however, a reference to the spring and the spring branch, but instead of being measured, in the picturesque fashion of the old-timers, from tree to tree, the distances are reckoned from stake to stake, and the symbolic hickory tree is dropped from the legal record of the boundaries.

This last recorded deed of the property, which appears on Page 149, Book 24, at the Davidson County Court House, reads in part: "... the following parcel of land situate in said county and State and being part of the late residence of Andrew Jackson deceased, containing by survey of Jesse B. Clements, Esquire, five hundred acres of land counted as follows, viz., Beginning at a stake on the northwest corner of A. H. Kerr's formerly Col. William Ward's land running thence East with his North boundary line, crossing the Lebanon Turnpike Road at one hundred and twenty-nine (129) poles in all two hundred and ten (210) poles to a stake in the West boundary line of A. J. Donelson's land thence North six and a half (6½) degrees East with his line one hundred and fifty six (156) poles to the Road aforesaid Thence North four (4) degrees East with said line thirty (30) poles thence North one (1) degree still in the Donelson's line East thirty three (33) poles to a Stake thence South eighty-eight (88) degrees West passing three poles North of the Spring and Stone spring house at one hundred and forty two (142) poles in all two hundred and thirty six (236) poles to a stake in William Donelson's East boundary line thence South one and a half (1½) degrees East with his line ninety four 94 poles to a Stake one of his corners thence West with another line of said William Donelson one hundred and eighteen poles to a Stake on the East Side of a Small branch thence North fifty nine (59) degrees West crossing said branch sixty one (61) poles to a Stake thence South with another line of said William Donelson two hundred and twelve poles (212) to a Stake thence East one hundred and seventy five and a half (175½) poles to a Stake in said Kerr's West boundary line, thence North (1½) one and a half degrees West with said line sixty five and a half (65½) poles to the beginning corner and including the late mansion, Tomb, Spring and Spring House, Barn and Stables of Genl. Andrew Jackson, deceased, as will more fully appear by reference to the plat at the head of this deed which is made part thereof...."

Before Andrew Jackson moved to the Hermitage, he lived on a near-by estate known as "Hunter's Hill." It is well, however, before going into the history of his home on this property, to trace briefly his residences from the time of his arrival in Davidson County in the fall of 1788.

We are legally informed of his presence and the beginning of his professional duties by the statement in Minute Book A, Davidson County Court, under the date of January 5, 1789, to the effect that "Andrew Jackson Esquire produced a licence to practice as an attorney at law in the Severall County courts in this State: and now in this court has taken the Oath of an Attorney."

Young Attorney Jackson, then in his twenty-first year, had come West to make his fortune. With him was John McNairy, who had but recently been appointed judge of the Superior Court of North Carolina's western district. John Overton, another young lawyer, had come West from Virginia by way of Kentucky, and it soon happened that he and young Jackson found common quarters at the home of the Widow Donelson. The young men were fortunate, for fare in such a home as Mrs. Donelson's was far better than that in the few stations or military posts which offered the only other shelter for young unattached men. Many of the families still lived in the stations and, in the most severe periods of Indian hostilities, every home which was not a well-manned fortress was abandoned. Mrs. Donelson had come to the Cumberland settlement in 1780 with her husband, Col. John Donelson, commander of the pioneer flotilla which brought the families of the first settlers to the site of Nashville. They arrived April 24, 1780, with their large family and slaves, and settled on the now famous "Clover Bottom" tract on Stone's River. Summer and autumn of that year, however, brought serious difficulties. Indians had attacked the settlement, food was scarce, crops had been lost in an overflow, and Col. Donelson was faced with the necessity of returning to the east on business for himself and other settlers. His large family was a serious responsibility and, rather than leave them without his protection he took them, in the fall of 1780, to the Kentucky settlement, where food was more plentiful, and where they would not be such a burden to the other settlers. The residence of the Donelson family until 1785 was in the neighborhood of Harrodsburg, but Col. Donelson, his older sons, and his sons-in-law, were engaged in various activities which kept them in motion up and down the western frontier from Natchez to the Cumberland and Harrodsburg. They were preparing, however, to take up a permanent residence in the Cumberland in 1785 when Col. Donelson, on his way from Kentucky to the Cumberland settlement, met a mysterious death, either at the hands of the Indians or two young white men who were, for a part of his journey, his companions.

Mrs. Donelson and her sons, however, had established themselves on lands in the Cumberland settlement. The home of Mrs. Donelson was on the opposite side of the river from Jones' Bend, in which Jackson was later to own lands and at the entrance of which his Hermitage was to be located. About the time of Jackson's arrival on the Cumberland, Mrs. Donelson was forced to send to Kentucky to bring her daughter, Rachel, who, in 1785, had been married to Lewis Robards, of Mercer f9 County, to the protection of the parental roof. Young Mrs. Robards had been made desperately unhappy by the ill nature and unjust suspicions of her husband and he, in a fit of temper, ordered her to leave his home. No sooner had she been carried to Tennessee by her brother than the husband became repentant and John Overton, who had boarded at the Robards' home in Kentucky and was familiar with both families, assumed the rôle of peacemaker. Consequently a reconciliation was brought about and Robards came to live at Mrs. Donelson's, with the avowed intention of not repeating his unfair treatment of his young wife and the apparent determination to make his home in the Cumberland. At any rate, in July, 1788, he acquired two important tracts of land in the neighborhood. The first was a tract of something over a thousand acres, purchased from William Mabane. It was, according to the deed, "A certain tract or parcel of land situate lying and being in Green County and State aforesaid on the West fork of Big Harpeth River...." The consideration was "the sum of two hundred pounds current money." (Davidson County was taken off of a portion of Greene County.)

The other tract, which by a peculiar turn of fate was to become the property of Andrew Jackson, was later known as "Hunter's Hill." This tract was granted to Lewis Robards by the State of North Carolina on the tenth day of July, 1788. It was sold by him for two hundred pounds to John Shannon on March 19, 1794— a significant fact, for on January 17, 1794, Andrew Jackson's second marriage to Rachel, Robards' divorced wife, took place. It is evident that Lewis Robards had no further interest in lands in Tennessee.

In the time which intervened between Robards' arrival at Mrs. Donelson's in 1788 and his final departure for Kentucky in May or June, 1790, the old story of the jealous husband was repeated. This time Andrew Jackson was the target of his anger and unjust suspicions, just as another young man—one Peyton Short—had been back in Kentucky. The incidents of this period are well known. As the breach between Robards and his wife widened, Jackson and Overton removed to Mansker's Station and, finally, Robards set out for Kentucky alone, threatening, however, to return and to force Rachel to go back to Kentucky with him. To escape him she fled to friends in Natchez either late in the year of 1790 or early in 1791, and Andrew Jackson went along to help protect the party against the Indians. Later news came to the Cumberland that a divorce had been granted Robards by the Virginia legislature in an act passed December 20, 1790, and Jackson hastened to Natchez to woo the unhappy Rachel. They were married in Natchez in August, 1791, and returned to Nashville in September. It was not until December, 1793, that Robards revealed the fact that the Virginia legislature had granted him only the right to sue for divorce in the courts of Kentucky. He exercised that right in the Mercer County court, term of September, 1793, and in the following December John Overton brought to the astounded Jackson the news that the Natchez marriage had not been legal. The second marriage took place openly, and though the circumstances which necessitated it were deplored by friends of the Jacksons, the situation was fully understood and no blame was attached to either of them.

About the time of the second marriage the Jacksons were probably living on a tract of land in "Jones' Bent" known as Poplar Grove. There is little known of this period, but a letter of Jackson's, dated May 16, 1794, is headed "Poplar Grove, Tenn." This tract, bought from John Donelson for the sum of one hundred pounds, April 30, 1793, was, according to the deed recorded at the Davidson County Court House, located on "the lower end of a survey of 630 acres granted the said John Donelson by patent." It is described as being "on the south side of Cumberland River in Jones Bent and bounded as follows— Beginning at sugar tree red oak and elm on the bank of the river, the lower end of the tract running thence north sixty degrees...."

MRS. RACHEL JACKSON

Mrs. Jackson's likeness is from the miniature which General Jackson wore every day until his death.

GENERAL ANDREW JACKSON

His is from the well-known military portrait by Earl.

The next important purchase from the standpoint of Jackson's homestead was that of the Hunter's Hill tract from John Shannon on March 7, 1796, "for and in consideration of the sum of seven hundred dollars to him in hand paid by the said Andrew Jackson." It is impossible to trace definitely the residence of Rachel and Andrew during the years intervening between their marriage in the late summer of 1791 and the acquisition of the Hunter's Hill tract in 1796. They must, for a period at least, have lived with Mrs. Donelson, or in the household of some member of the family. Rachel had frequently lived at the home of her sister Jane, Mrs. Robert Hays, of Haysborough—once the rival of Nashville. A study of Indian hostilities of the period indicates that permanent residence outside the strongholds of the community was not practical. In 1792 Buchanan's station was attacked by a party of several hundred Indians, and as late as September, 1794, five men were fired upon by the Indians "near Mr. Andrew Jackson's, on the south side of Cumberland River." One was killed and two wounded.

Several things happened in 1794 which indicate that the Jacksons were established in a home of their own—the reference in a communication to the War Department to the Indian depredations "near Mr. Andrew Jackson's"; the previously mentioned letter, which Jackson himself headed "Poplar Grove, Tenn. May 16, 1794;" and freedom from Indian attacks on outlying settlements. The important Nickajack expedition, which brought an end to all organized Indian hostilities in the section, took place in that year.

The death of Mrs. Jackson's mother, Rachel Stockley Donelson, which, according to a marker erected a few years ago by members of the Donelson family, occurred in 1794, was offered in the first edition of the present work as another reason that Andrew and Rachel Jackson had gone into a home of their own. This seems to be in error. As far as the writer knows at present, the date of her death has not been established. However, it was after October 2, 1800. (See pp. 491-92, *General Jackson's Lady*, by Mary French Caldwell.)

The Nickajack expedition was noteworthy, not only for the success of its immediate objects, but also for its effectiveness in bringing a lasting peace to the frontiers, and for the fact that it was conducted in defiance of the Federal government. The territorial governor, William Blount, in a letter to General Knox, Secretary of War, written in Knoxville, October 2, 1794, recites the sufferings of the inhabitants in the "district of Mero" and tells of depredations which took place while the frontiersmen were on their way to the Cherokee Lower Towns—Nickajack, Running Water, and others of lesser importance.

> "While Major Ore was out against the Lower Town," he wrote, "the Indians continued their depredations against the district of Mero. On the night of the fourteenth September, the Indians pulled up a part of the stockading of Morgan's station, and took out a valuable gelding tied to his dwelling house. The sixteenth of the same month, a woman on Red river near Major Sharp's was killed by the Indians. The same day a party of Indians fired upon five men near Mr. Andrew Jackson's, on the south side of Cumberland river, killed one man, and wounded two; among the latter is Mr. John Bosley. The same party burned the houses of John Donnelson and the widow Hayes. From the nearness of the time, and the distance of the situation, within which the above injuries were committed, there must have been three parties of Indians." (*Indian Affairs*, Vol. I, page 663.)

The Nickajack expedition began on September 8, 1794, so at the time that these depredations took place the settlement was in an unprotected condition. Since before the Civil War Andrew Jackson's participation in this campaign has been a matter of dispute. The historian Ramsey, in his *Annals of Tennessee*, said that he served as a private; but Putnam, in his work on Middle Tennessee, basing his statement on the word of men who participated in the expedition, declares that he did not go. Putnam is followed by Parton and, since both of them have so vehemently denied that he had a part in it, this position has been almost generally accepted.

Ramsey based his statement on papers of Willie Blount, half brother of the territorial governor, who, at the time was secretary of the territory, and was later himself governor of Tennessee. Both Putnam and Parton have failed to take into consideration the importance of Blount's testimony—or, perhaps, did not have access to his papers. A letter which should settle the controversy permanently has been recently acquired by the state historian and librarian, Mrs. John Trotwood Moore. This letter, written to General Jackson on January 4, 1830, by Willie Blount, states:

> "I have by me the rough draft of sundry letters, from me to you, none of which have yet been either copied or mailed: they relate to things gone bye, & so, no matter whether they are ever sent or not: they speak only of the pleasurable feelings I

experience in the knowledge I possess of the motives and conduct in the various promotions of my friend yourself and the result of your efforts since the battle of Nickajack, commanded by Orr: where, as Sampson Williams says, our friend, the Mountain Leader, the friend of man, was at that never to be forgotten good days work, in which you lent an active useful hand, that gave peace to our frontier, never to be forgotten by me."

It is fitting that this letter should be published for the first time in a volume on the Hermitage, for it is an interesting contribution to the incomplete records of Andrew Jackson's early career in Tennessee. It is not strange, of course, that these records should be scant. Jackson was too young, too busy, and too completely unaware of the greatness which awaited him to have an interest in preserving personal records of this early period. Certainly his acquaintances could not have seen in the tall, slender, red-haired young attorney a future president and a great general.

Many disconnected court records may be found. A few of his account books survive and some of his letters have escaped oblivion; but, for the most part, the records of his early military activities, his mercantile business, and his land deals are incomplete. It is impossible to quote in detail from the court records of his land deals—that would require a separate volume. It is possible to show from them, however, that when he owned both the Hunter's Hill and Hermitage tracts, his holdings in the Hermitage neighborhood totaled something like 1,200 acres. The extent of his land fluctuated from time to time with his changing fortunes. For instance he sold the Hunter's Hill tract in 1804, bought it back at a later period of prosperity, and sold it again under financial pressure. At his death he held a plantation in Mississippi, as well as his Hermitage estate and adjoining lands bought from the heirs of Savern Donelson.

The Hermitage estate, as described by Andrew Jackson himself on September 30, 1841 (Bassett, Correspondence of Andrew Jackson, Vol. VI, p. 125) was as follows:

"The following is the boundery of my Hermitage track and its appendages, viz, Beginning at a stake, Andrew Jacksons South East corner, on Major A. J. Donelsons west boundery line and Mrs. Wards North East corner, running line thence North Eight east with A. J. Donelson to a post oak near A. J. Donelsons gate, then West to the turn pike road, then with the turn pike road to the old road leading to James Saunders ferry, thence North with A. J. Donelsons line to an ash and Locust, then East with his line to a black oak, thence North with his line to the North boundery line of Hugh Hays premption, thence West with the old preemption line to a stone, the North West corner of Hugh Hays preemption thence south with this preemption line, passing a walnutt corner, (the South West and North West corner of said Hugh Hays, and Nathaniel Hays preemption) continued South with said N. Hays line to the mouth of the lane leading to Wm. Donelsons to a cedar stake, the North east corner of Savern Donelsons 640 acres that *he died* seized of and the South east corner of William Donelsons land, thence West along the old line to a cedar stake, corner to A. Jackson and William Donelson, thence down the meanders of a branch to a stone corner, thence south with Wm. Donelsons line, passing his corner, and with T. Dodsons line to a white ash at Dodsons fence, then East with Dodsons line, and Mrs. Wards line to an Elm, then North with Mrs. Wards line to a dogwood, Andrew Jacksons corner, thence East to the beginning, containing in all nine hundred and sixty acres. I send you the exterior boundery of my whole tract...."

His holdings in other parts of the territory which is now Tennessee were almost as limitless as the wilderness itself. Like the other leaders of the period—although on a somewhat smaller scale than his brother-in-law, Stockley Donelson, William Blount, and John Sevier—he dealt in great bodies of wild lands. One interesting thing that Jackson's records show is that he was remarkably successful in many of his deals, particularly in the smaller ones which had to do with the exchange of lands in the neighborhood of Nashville. It is extremely interesting to observe that on March 19, 1794, Lewis Robards sold the future Hunter's Hill tract to John Shannon for the sum of two hundred pounds; that on March 7, 1796, Andrew Jackson bought it of Shannon for seven hundred dollars; and that on July 6, 1804, Jackson sold it to Edward Ward for $10,000. A rough estimate of sixteen land deals recorded in Davidson County in Books C and D shows that between May 3, 1793, and February 18, 1797, he had bought something like twenty-seven thousand acres of land at an expenditure of about $20,000. These records show his major transactions of this period for two very obvious reasons—the land to the east was already largely taken up and the land in the major portion of what is now Middle Tennessee, as well as that in the future West Tennessee, was recorded in Davidson County. These deals are catalogued briefly as follows:

Book C

Page 134—Approximately 630 acres of John Donelson, in Jones' Bent, for 100 pounds, August 30, 1793.

Page 140—320 acres of James Robertson and Hugh Leeper, on north side of Duck River, on Leeper's Creek, for 100 pounds currency, May 3, 1793.

Page 242—640 acres of Edward Cox of Sullivan county, in Davidson County on east branches of Mill Creek, for 500 pounds, February 11, 1794.

Page 316—Buys as highest bidder, for eleven pounds, 640 acres on Big Harpeth joining Governor Martin's survey, August 2, 1794. (Land recovered at July court, 1793, by Henry Bradford against Lardner Clark.)

Page 492—5,000 acres for $400, bought of Joseph B. Neville, Sheriff of Tennessee County, a tract of land on Reelfoot River, the property of the heirs of Henry Boyer, which had been advertised for forty days and sold at Clarksville to Sheriff Neville, who represented Andrew Jackson and was the highest bidder. April 18, 1796.

Page 493—250 acres for $60 sold to Andrew Jackson by Thomas Hickman. Located "on the south side of Tennessee River, some small distance from where a hurricane hath crossed said river...." Recorded April 18, 1796.

Page 495—640 acres for the "sum of six pence an acre" from Reese Porter, "in the Middle District lying on the South side of Duck River on the waters of Lytle's Creek." April 19, 1796.

Page 495—640 acres for $700, of John Shannon, Logan County, Kentucky, "a certain tract or parcel of land containing 640 acres ... situate and lying in the said county of Davidson on Cumberland river on the south side ... it being a premption grant to Lewis Robards by grant from the State of North Carolina, bearing date of July tenth 1788." March 7, 1796. (This is the Hunter's Hill tract.)

Page 496—1,000 acres for $250, in the Western District of Tennessee, on the waters of the north fork of Deer River, bought of William Terrell Lewis. March 11, 1796.

Page 497—525 acres for $5.25, part of 1,280-acre tract belonging to "one George Augustus Sugg." Sold at Sheriff's sale, December 8, 1795.

BOOK D

Page 42—5,000 acres for $2,500, "in the Middle District on the Middle fork of Elk River," bought of Elijah Robertson, May 14, 1796.

Page 43—5,160 acres for $6,000, composed of twelve tracts of land, much of which had been granted to Elijah Robertson by the State of North Carolina, May 14, 1796.

Page 48—"One undivided half or moiety of a tract of land on Chickasaw Bluff, beginning about one mile below the mouth of Wolf River, which s^d tract was granted to John Rice by patent bearing date the 25th day of April 1789," bought of John Overton for $100, February 28, 1796.

Page 108—640 acres for $540, in Sumner County on South Side of the Cumberland and on "Spencer's Creek, including the Lick," bought of Joseph Hendricks, February 18, 1797.

Page 454—2,560 acres for $2,000, four tracts of 640 acres each in Sumner County, bought of Martin Armstrong and Stockley Donelson, May 9, 1796.

Page 455—3200 acres from $3,000, five tracts in Sumner County, bought of Martin Armstrong and Stockley Donelson, May 9, 1796.

Page 455—1,000 acres for $1,000, "in the middle district on the North side of Duck River, Opposite the mouth of Lick Creek, known by some by the name of Sugar Creek ..." bought of Stockley Donelson, May 9, 1796.

BOOK F

Page 70—10,000 acres for $182. On April 19, 1802, "at the Court House in the Town of Nashville 85,000 acres of land contained in grants for 5,000 acres each ... lying and being on Duck River in the Middle District and within the District of West (now Middle) Tennessee aforesaid which sixteen tracts were granted to John Gray Blount and Thomas Blount by them conveyed to David Allison deceased and by said David Allison in his lifetime mortgaged to Norton Pryor and ordered and decreed by said court to be sold to pay the mortgage money and Interest with

Costs, and whereas Andrew Jackson Esquire at said sale became purchaser of two of said tracts for five thousand acres each ... for the sum of $182 ... he being the highest and last bidder ... and whereas the said Andrew Jackson has sold and transferred all his right in and to one of said tracts of 5,000 acres ... to John Overton and Jenkin Whiteside for the Consideration of $1,666.66 to him paid and secured ... upon the condition that the said Andrew is not to be answerable in any way or manner for Damages or the Consideration Money in case the Land should be Lost or Taken away by any Claim or Title whatever...." April 25, 1802.

Page 188—Sold to Edward Ward 640 acres for $10,000, July 6, 1804. (This was the Hunter's Hill tract bought from John Shannon on March 7, 1796, for $700.)

Page 241—425 acres for $3,400, bought of Nathaniel Hays (ancestor of the late John Hays Hammond), August 23, 1804. (The Hermitage tract, which sold to the State of Tennessee in 1856 for the sum of $48,000.)

Book E records the purchase of 1,000 acres for $500, and this with the deals mentioned in Book F adds 11,425 acres to the total of 27,825 acres mentioned in deeds between 1793 and 1797, making a grand total of 39,250 acres. These eighteen transactions show that for most of the land Jackson paid a reasonably good price for the period, and that sometimes he made a fabulous profit. This study by no means gives a complete picture of his land deals, but it gives an idea of his major deals at the period of his greatest activity in this field. There never was a time in his life when records of his personal business would not show some activity in the purchase or sale of land.

His mercantile business, which is quite as interesting, was confined to the earlier period of his life in Tennessee. It began about 1795 and ended, tradition says, in 1809, when as a wedding gift to General John Coffee, his former partner, he tore up the notes which he held on the Clover Bottom store.

As early as 1795 we find Andrew Jackson in partnership with David Allison in a shipment of goods from Philadelphia to Nashville. Five years earlier Allison, Jackson, Overton, and others were licensed to practice law in the new territory by Governor William Blount, and various records show Allison's activities in Davidson County, as well as in Philadelphia, where he was a well-known merchant. From this connection and subsequent associations in both land and mercantile deals developed a relationship which was finally to force Jackson to sell his handsome Hunter's Hill tract in order to meet his obligations. It is a long and complicated story, and its chief importance in the present connection is that responsibility for Jackson's loss of Hunter's Hill and his removal to more humble quarters on the Hermitage estate is usually attributed to the Allison deal. It is a significant fact, however, that Allison's failure, which occurred about 1795, did not result in the sale of Hunter's Hill until July 6, 1804. It is reasonable, then, to suppose that it by no means crippled Jackson, as most writers contend; although it undoubtedly marked the beginning of a long struggle through a period of financial unrest and depression which resulted finally in a plan of retrenchment and reorganization.

THE LOG HERMITAGE—1805

The building in the foreground was once a two-story block-house.

THE BRICK HERMITAGE—1819

Wings were added in 1831, and the small building was removed. *From Harper's Magazine of January, 1855*

On the twenty-third of August, 1804, Jackson paid Nathaniel Hays $3,400 for the 425-acre tract, "with its appurtenances," which was to be known later as the Hermitage.[1] This reference to appurtenances would indicate that some kind of a building or "improvements" stood on the property when Jackson bought it. This theory is strengthened by the fact that the present study has revealed no records which prove definitely that Andrew Jackson erected a log building at the Hermitage in 1804 or 1805, and by the tradition in the Hays family that one of its members built the Hermitage. Another point which strengthens it is that both of the log houses now standing on the Hermitage estate have in their walls the customary holes for rifles which were made in the days of Indian fighting. This was not necessary at the time Jackson bought the Hermitage, for Indian hostilities were ended by 1795.

There must have been, however, considerable remodeling of the buildings, even though no new house was erected. Account books of the Hunter's Hill store, which form a valuable part of the collection of historic documents at the Hermitage, show that in November, 1804, "17 window lights" are charged to Jackson's personal account. It is possible that as time goes by a letter or other record may come to light which will tell something more definite on the building or remodeling of the log Hermitage. These account books are especially important in placing the removal from Hunter's Hill to the Hermitage. The last entry at the Hunter's Hill store was made on April 5, 1805, and the first at the Clover Bottom store on April 9. It is interesting to observe in this connection that the first letter in Bassett's *Correspondence of Andrew Jackson*, headed at the Hermitage, was dated April 7, 1805. There is a lapse of several months in the letters, however, since the last one Bassett quotes from Hunter's Hill is dated August 25, 1804. It is probable, although not a definitely established fact, that the removal of the store and residence took place simultaneously.

It is known, of course, that Hunter's Hill was a commodious, two-story frame building—a marked contrast with the usual log houses of the period. In later years it was burned, and there remains to-day on the site of the Hunter's Hill residence nothing more than a few scant traces of houses which may, or may not, have been a part of the dwellings, slave quarters, store, or other buildings used while the Jacksons lived there.[2] The spring, of course, remains; the Cumberland flows gently along its distant, tree-lined banks; and fertile fields still yield up their annual tribute to careful husbandry. But marks of Jackson's occupation of the land are obliterated and, except as the story is pieced together from bits of information gathered here and there, its history is lost in obscurity.

More is known of the log Hermitage, although its history is far from complete. Most of the letters of people who were guests of the Jacksons during this period are tantalizing for their lack of detail. The best and more than likely the most authentic description of the interior of the log Hermitage is that given in Buell's *History of Andrew Jackson*. The author, in a series of interviews with Mrs. James K. Polk, wife of President Polk, has preserved much important material relating to the Jackson household. In his preface to Mrs. Polk's narrative he says:

> "In the early seventies of the 19th Century the author of this work visited Nashville more than once in the capacity of a newspaper correspondent. On those occasions he enjoyed the honor and pleasure of calling upon Mrs. Sarah Childress Polk, widow of the President. Mrs. Polk was in her seventy-first year then. Her fund of historical and social reminiscences was

exhaustless, and the best efforts to reproduce in print her faculty of relation would be feeble. Born in 1803, about twenty-eight or thirty miles from Nashville and not over twenty miles from the Hermitage, she had known the Jacksons from her earliest childhood. When she grew up and married Mr. Polk, the intimacy became still closer, and the relations between General Jackson and her husband in public life on the most important scale gave her recollections a quality of historical value not equalled by those of any other woman of her time....

"Mrs. Polk said that Mrs. Jackson—or 'Aunt' Rachel—was literally the childless mother of the whole neighborhood.... In their vicinage General and Mrs. Jackson were, of course, by far the most important persons. But no one would suspect it from observing the way and manner of their intercourse with the neighbors. In this respect the General was the most democratic of men, while Mrs. Jackson was at once the soul of merry-making and the embodiment of benevolence and charity.

"Their home manners, Mrs. Polk said, were the most charming concert of simplicity with dignity. The General always in their earlier life said 'Mrs. Jackson,' both in the second and third persons; though, when their little adopted son began to talk, he got into the habit of addressing her as 'mother.' On her part, Mrs. Jackson invariably spoke of and to him as 'Mr. Jackson,' until after the War of 1812, she yielded to the universal fashion and began to call him 'General.' But no one ever heard either address the other by the first name or by any term of endearment or familiarity whatever. In fact, though more winning kindliness than that which marked the manners of both could not be imagined, there was yet an atmosphere of quiet self-respect and calm dignity about them which gently, though none the less imperatively, commanded scrupulous courtesy in their presence....

"The Hermitage of the period now under consideration, Mrs. Polk said, was not the commodious country house so familiar to devout Democrats in pilgrimages of later years. It was a group of log houses in close proximity to each other. The principal one had been built for a block-house in the days of Indian alarms, afterwards used as a store and, about 1804, converted into a dwelling. It, like all block-houses, was two stories high. Near it were three smaller log houses, one story high with low attics. These were used as lodgings for members of the family or guests. The main building—the former blockhouse—had on the first floor one very large room with a huge fireplace capable of taking in a good-sized load of wood at a time. A lean-to had been built on at the back containing two rooms, one of which was used as the family sleeping quarters, the other as a pantry—or 'buttery' as the phrase was then. But the great room, about twenty-four feet by twenty-six, was at once kitchen, dining-room, sitting-room and parlor, and the large table that stood in the middle of it, capable of seating twelve to fourteen people comfortably, was always 'set.'

"... General Jackson was a wonderful adept in the art of anecdote, and particularly delighted in incidents having a spice of wit or humor. Mrs. Jackson's observations and experience were, of course, much more limited, but she, too, was a fluent talker and always entertaining.... She was an insatiable reader and was always far better informed upon current topics than the average woman of her time, even those who had been well educated. She was also a prolific writer, keeping up a close correspondence with her numerous relatives and with the General whenever he was absent from home. Her letters were simply her conversation on paper, with no effort at eloquence. As for grammar and orthography, Mrs. Polk said, neither in those days was the exact science it has since become, and she declared that while in the White House she had received notes from 'leaders in society' in Washington that would not compare favorably with the most hurried or careless of Mrs. Jackson's letters."

Mrs. Polk was excellently educated for her time. As a very young girl she was sent to the Moravian Female Academy at Salem, North Carolina, and later she was placed in a girls' school in Nashville. She came, of course, a generation after Mrs. Jackson and enjoyed privileges which were not known in frontier days. Mrs. Polk's estimate of the Jacksons is especially important, not only because she knew them intimately from her childhood, but also because by training and long contact with the nation's leaders and the great from other parts of the world, she had a background which qualified her for unbiased judgment.

Another child destined for future greatness visited the Hermitage when the log buildings were the family dwellings. He was Jefferson Davis, future president of the Confederate States of America. What would "Old Hickory" have said, when little "Jeff" Davis raced ponies and played with Andrew Jackson, Jr., and other little boys at the Hermitage, had he been able to foretell the future of his small guest? Fortunately for the children, no shadow crossed their pathway, and even "Old Hickory" had not been forced to declare in thunderous tones: "Our Federal Union—it must be preserved."

[Let it always be remembered, however, that Andrew Jackson's passionate loyalty to the Union was based upon an equally passionate devotion to the Rights of the States. He said in a rough draft of his second inaugural address, dated March 1, 1833 (Bassett, *Correspondence of Andrew Jackson*, Vol. V, p. 26): "In proportion, therefore, as the general government encroaches upon the rights of the states, in the same proportion does it impair its own power and detract from its ability to fulfil the purposes of its creation."]

The story of Jefferson Davis' journey from Mississippi to the Hermitage is told briefly in his *Memoirs*.

"When I was seven years old," he states, "I was sent on horseback through what was then called 'The Wilderness'—by the country of the Choctaw and the Chickasaw nations—to Kentucky, and placed in a Catholic institution then known as St. Thomas, in Washington County, near the town of Springfield. In that day (1815) there were no steamboats, nor were there stage-coaches traversing the country. The river trade was conducted on flat and keel-boats. The last named only could be taken up the river. Commerce between the Western States and the Lower Mississippi was confined to the water routes. The usual mode of travel was on horseback or afoot. Many persons who had gone down the river in flat-boats walked back through the wilderness to Kentucky, Ohio, and elsewhere. We passed many of these, daily, on the road....

"The party with which I was sent to Kentucky consisted of Major Hinds (who had command of the famous battalion of Mississippi dragoons at the battle of New Orleans), his wife, his sister-in-law, a niece, a maid-servant, and his son Howell, who was near my own age, and, like myself, mounted on a pony. A servant had a sumpter mule with some supplies, besides bed and blankets for camping out. The journey to Kentucky occupied several weeks.

"When we reached Nashville we went to the Hermitage. Major Hinds wished to visit his friend and companion-in-arms,

General Jackson. The whole party was so kindly received that we remained several weeks. During that period I had the opportunity a boy has to observe a great man—a standpoint of no small advantage—and I have always remembered with warm affection the kind and tender wife who then presided over his house....

"General Jackson's house at that time was a roomy log-house. In front of it was a grove of fine forest trees, and behind it were his cotton and grain fields. I have never forgotten the unaffected and well-bred courtesy which caused him to be remarked by court-trained diplomats, when President of the United States, by reason of his very impressive bearing and manner. Notwithstanding the many reports that have been made of his profanity, I remember that he always said grace at his table and I never heard him utter an oath. In the same connection, although he encouraged his adopted son, A. Jackson, Jr., Howell Hinds, and myself in all contests of activity, pony-riding included, he would not allow us to wrestle; for, he said, to allow hands to be put on one another might lead to a fight. He was always very gentle and considerate.... Our stay with General Jackson was enlivened by the visits of his neighbors, and we left the Hermitage with great regret and pursued our journey. In me he inspired reverence and affection that has remained with me through my whole life."

These intimate glimpses of the Jackson household during the period of residence in the log Hermitage throw an interesting light upon the customs and surroundings of the family at this time. These years—from 1805 to 1819—were tremendously important in Jackson's career. They were not entirely happy years, for they included such unfortunate events as the Dickinson duel in 1806, the shooting affray with the Bentons in 1814, the delightful, but misunderstood visits of Aaron Burr, and the public expressions of disapproval which these affairs produced. Through it all ran the unhappy references to the Robards' divorce and the unfortunate circumstances attending the first marriage of the Jacksons. It was a period of Herculean struggle against material odds, as well as against public opinion, but it was not without a brighter side in which gayety, color, and genuine happiness stand out.

Relatives, neighbors and, often, distinguished guests from a distance, composed a brilliant and congenial company—in spite of the fact that their rank varied from the simplest backwoodsman to a former vice president of the United States, and their common background was a log house in the far west. Most charming and gracious of all was Aaron Burr, but lately vice president, who first visited the Hermitage May 29, 1805. He was received by the entire community in a manner which befitted his importance and his high rank in national affairs. Public dinners were given for him, and he was received cordially by the leading citizens. He returned to Nashville in August, 1805, and spent a few days as a guest of General Jackson. Little is known of the details of this visit, but from the Hermitage at this time he wrote to his daughter, Theodosia:

> "For a week I have been lounging at the house of General Jackson, once a lawyer, after a judge, now a planter; a man of intelligence, and one of those prompt, frank, ardent souls whom I love to meet. The General has no children, but two lovely nieces made a visit of some days, contributed greatly to my amusement, and have cured me of all the evils of my wilderness jaunt...." (Parton's *Life of Andrew Jackson.*)

The nieces were, of course, nieces of Mrs. Jackson—part of that bevy of charming Donelson girls which throughout the history of the Hermitage household lent grace and gayety to its social affairs. Many of them married young men who were closely associated with the General in his military and political activities, and in this way strengthened by ties of kinship the relationship which common public interest had created. General Jackson had no kin of his own in Tennessee, but he took Mrs. Jackson's family to his heart as if it were his own.

Burr's final visit to Nashville in December, 1806, was the one around which the storm of public disapproval centered. His reception at this time was courteous, but somewhat cool, for rumors of his proposed invasion of the West had already begun to filter in. The *Impartial Review and Cumberland Repository* of December 20 carried the announcement that "Colo. Burr arrived on Wednesday last and intends proceeding to Natchez in a few days."

His departure was recorded almost as briefly in the same paper, issue of Saturday, December 27: "Colo. Burr embarked from this place for New Orleans on Monday last, with two large flat boats, which did not appear to be loaded."

The papers of these and subsequent dates carried, however, many communications which show the national alarm at Burr's presence in the Western country and indicate that while Nashville was slow to condemn him, it was ready to rise to a man to march against him should reports that he was planning an invasion of the Western country prove true. For the most part, however, he was given the benefit of the doubt, and while he was in Nashville he was received as an interesting and charming acquisition to its social circle.

There are many interesting stories of Burr's visits to Nashville, of his elegant manners, his wit, and his personal magnetism as well as his alleged duplicity. Some of them were revived in the Jackson presidential campaign of 1828 in an effort to prove that he and Andrew Jackson were united in intrigue against the United States. These arguments brought forth a letter which was not only important in the campaign, but is especially valuable at present, for its picture of Nashville social life and the participation of the master and mistress of the Hermitage in it. This letter, written by T. G. Watkins, at Charlottesville, on May 14, 1828, reads:

> "In the winter of 1806 or '7, to the best of my recollection as to time, I was a member of the dancing assemblies for the season, in Nashville. On one of the evenings preceding a stated meeting for the night, it was communicated to the managers for the season, two of whom I distinctly recollect were the present John Overton, LLD, of Travellers' Rest, near Nashville, and the late Dr. Hansen Catlett, that Col. Burr was in town. He was immediately ticketed, as Judge Overton informed me, nem. con., I think, by the managers. Some one, I do not now recollect who, objected to this act of the managers. Judge Overton remarked that he had concurred in the invitation from a conviction of its propriety—but, as he acted upon delegated authority, he wished a meeting as full and general as practicable, of the subscribers to the assemblies to be convened; and if a majority of them disapproved of the act of the managers, the invitation to Mr. Burr should be promptly withdrawn. A meeting, a very full meeting, was called, and a majority sanctioned the act of the managers. The ball went on very harmoniously; Col. Burr, though somewhat distrusted by some, was considered an elegant acquisition to it, and was treated accordingly: a hospitable and gracious smile from the ladies, in return for his very general, and very elegant salutations, proved their happy acquiescence in the general

arrangement. Gen. Jackson resided about 14 miles from Nashville at that time: if he and his amiable lady attended on that occasion, as they often did on others, I have lost all distinct recollection of it, which I think I should not, if there had been anything more marked in the attention of either to Col. Burr than seemed to be generally awarded to him by the company. While on this subject I will remark that some time previous to this ball, a young gentleman who resided in my family in Nashville, appeared anxious to go with Col. Burr—he afterwards cooled off. And questioned on the subject by myself or someone in my presence, he stated that a Mr. Caffrey, I think was the name, had been about that time advised, verbally or by letter, I am not certain which, by Gen. Jackson, to have nothing to do with Col. Burr's expedition. Respectfully Th. G. Watkins." (*Nashville Whig*.)

Above: THE HERMITAGE AFTER THE REMODELLING IN 1831
From Ayres' Map of Nashville Courtesy of the late Dr. W. A. Provine

Below: THE HERMITAGE AFTER THE FINAL REMODELLING
WHICH FOLLOWED THE FIRE OF 1834

From drawing dated 1856 Original in Hermitage museum

Burr, on his last visit to Nashville, resided at least a part of the time at the Clover Bottom tavern, which, with a store, a race track, and a boat yard, formed the establishment developed by Andrew Jackson, John Hutchings, a nephew of Mrs. Jackson, and John Coffee, who in 1809 married one of Mrs. Jackson's nieces, Mary Donelson. It was here that Burr obtained the boats which brought down such a storm of criticism upon the head of Jackson. A careful examination of the orders for boats and related dealings between Jackson and Burr do not justify the accusation of conspiracy—particularly in view of General Jackson's activities in complying with orders from the Secretary of War regarding a military force to protect the West against Burr's anticipated invasion.

After Burr's departure with his two visibly empty flat-boats, feeling in certain circles began to mount higher and higher. He was publicly denounced as a traitor and on January 2, 1807, was burned in effigy by a group of Nashville's citizens. This event is described in the *Impartial Review* of Saturday, January 3, 1807, as follows:

> "Last night at the hour of nine, commenced the burning of the Effigy of Col. Aaron Burr, by the citizens of this town. This proceeding is justified by the ardent emotions of patriotism felt by the people, and excited by a deep conviction that the said Burr is a TRAITOR. This conviction is produced from the conduct of Col. Burr himself in these western states, and even in this town—the proclamation of the President—his message to both houses of Congress, and the statement of Gen. Eaton. And we have the utmost confidence in assuring our Atlantic brethren, that the idea of separation is spurned with indignation and horror. That our lives and our property are pledged to support the General Government of the United States, as the safeguard of our personal security, and as the only asylum for oppressed humanity."

Subsequent events proved that the Burr alarm was very much of a tempest in a teapot, but the incident was used, long afterwards, against General Jackson by his political opponents. Similar use was made of the Robards' divorce and of the tragic story of his duel with Charles Dickinson.

The log house was the home of the Jacksons at the time of the Dickinson duel, May 29, 1806; but the scene of events which led to it was Clover Bottom, the site of Jackson's race track, store, and tavern, about two miles from the Hermitage. The direct cause of the duel was the race between Jackson's celebrated Truxton and Capt. Joseph Erwin's Ploughboy—a race which was arranged in the fall of 1805, but was not run. Ploughboy's lameness caused his owner to withdraw him from the race and pay the $800 forfeit. There are a number of stories about events which followed the withdrawal of Ploughboy. Judge Guild, in his *Old Times in Tennessee*, probably gives the most accurate account of the matter as it concerns Mrs. Jackson.

> "I have been informed," Judge Guild wrote, "by a relative of Mrs. Jackson, a gentleman of high character, still living, that she was present, in her carriage, on the track, to witness the race, and when the forfeit was declared, she remarked with an air of pardonable exultation, to some of her friends, that 'Truxton would have left Ploughboy out of sight.' This was repeated to Dickinson, who, being somewhat excited by his losses, and probably under the influence of liquor, rejoined, 'Yes, about as far out of sight as Mrs. Jackson left her first husband when she ran away with the General.'"

This was followed by some gentlemen's gossip about the value of notes put up by Capt. Erwin for the forfeit, and one incrimination led to another until a situation which had but one remedy was created. Jackson, by the repeated insults heaped upon him by the Erwin faction, was forced to challenge Charles Dickinson to a duel. Since the laws of Tennessee prohibited dueling, the meeting was carried across the line into Kentucky, where, on the morning of May 29, 1806, the duel was fought. The results are well known. Dickinson, crack pistol shot of the West, who had left behind him along the road to the meeting place evidences of his expert marksmanship, fired—and the shot entered his adversary's breast. His opponent fired, but the pistol stopped at half-cock. With superhuman effort he drew himself to full height, folded his coat closer across his breast to hide the wound which he believed fatal, and with cool deliberation took the second fire to which he was entitled. Dickinson's wound proved fatal and Jackson's very nearly so, but the bitter enemies who had driven Jackson into the duel were not satisfied—they entered upon a relentless tirade of abuse, and the public, shuddering, turned its sympathy to the young widow of Dickinson. Rachel, in her little log house, wept out her own heartache as she nursed the General back to health—and through it all prayed and wept for the young wife of Charles Dickinson and her unborn babe.

(The first edition of the present work referred to the Dickinson child as an "unborn babe"—a statement which had long been accepted by Jackson historians. Charles Dickinson's will in *Wills and Inventories of Davidson County*, (1807) pp. 141-142, states, however, that "... half of my Estate I give devise & bequeath to my son Henry who is now about Ten weeks old ...")

As time passed the wound healed. Jackson retired to his Hermitage and devoted himself to his business, his farm, and his blooded stock. Truxton, the innocent cause of this tragedy, blossomed under the friendly skies of Tennessee, but neither he nor his master were destined to remain long in retirement. Life stretched out temptingly before them, and it was not long until Truxton was the acknowledged king of the turf, and upon his master's brow were the laurels won in his defense of New Orleans.

No history of the Hermitage could be complete without a rather detailed account of Truxton. He was bought by General Jackson in the spring of 1805 from Maj. John Verrell, of Virginia. After the first race with Ploughboy was announced and the forfeit declared, another race, which is less known, was run and Truxton was the winner. This race took place on April 3, 1806—something over a month before the Dickinson duel.

The best authority on this race and upon Truxton himself is Andrew Jackson. His statement was written for the *American Farmer* and was reprinted in the *American Turf Register* of December, 1833. This account reads:

> "Truxton is a beautiful bay, full of bone and muscle; was got by the imported horse old Diomed, and came out of the thoroughbred mare, Nancy Coleman, the property of Maj. John Verrell, of Virginia. Truxton is, however, too well known to require a minute description. His performances on the turf have surpassed those of any horse of his age that has ever been run in the western country; and, indeed, it might be said with confidence, that he is equal, if not superior, to Mr. Ball's Florizel horse, who was got by the same Diomed, and who now stands unrivalled in Virginia as a race horse.
>
> "Truxton, by old sportsmen and judges, is admitted to be amongst the best distance horses they ever run or had to train. His speed is certainly unknown to all those who have run against him. He has, on the most unequal terms, started against the very best mile horses in Kentucky and Tennessee, and beat them with great ease; and in no one instance has ever run with any horse, when he himself was in order, but he either could or did distance him with ease. Although the four mile heats is the real and true distance for Truxton to run, he has beaten Mr. Gordon's fine mile horse, Jack of Clubs, and Mr. Cotton's Greyhound, both aged horses, with equal weights of 100 pounds on each, the single mile heats.
>
> "And lastly, to crown the much doubted speed of Truxton, he beat, on only two sound legs, on the 3d of April, 1806, over the Clover Bottom Turf, the celebrated horse, Ploughboy, who was never before beaten, and beating him without the assistance of whip or spurs. It is now no longer difficult for the numerous concourse of people who were present on that day to say 'whether or not Truxton be the true bred racer.'
>
> "Truxton's winnings, from time to time, from the most correct information, amount to at least twenty thousand dollars, and his colts are not inferior to any on the continent. Andrew Jackson."[3]

Truxton was, undoubtedly, Jackson's pride, but the Hermitage was noted for many famous horses. There was Pacolet, the dapple gray six-year-old, which the General had bought from Col. William R. Johnson, of Kentucky, about 1813. His immediate object in acquiring a new racer was, according to Marquis James, in his *Andrew Jackson, the Border Captain*, to defeat "Jesse Haynie's chestnut mare Maria just as soon as he could send the British about their business." This neither Pacolet, nor Truxton's boasted colts could accomplish, and to Haynie's Maria is awarded the distinction of being almost the only thing which Andrew Jackson, when he set his head to it, could not conquer.

To tell the story of Jackson's horses would be to write the history of racing and breeding of thoroughbreds from the early days of the settlements in Middle Tennessee until after the Civil War. There was a close association between General Jackson and the owners of thoroughbreds in Sumner County, where, for a long period of years such men as Bailie Peyton, Barry, Carter, the Rev. Hardy Cryer and others produced magnificent horses.

There is a tradition that Andrew Jackson arrived in Nashville riding one fine horse and leading another—which was loaded in the customary manner with his personal belongings. Early in the spring after his arrival he purchased another, for we find at the Davidson County Court House a record showing that on April ninth, 1789, he bought of Thomas Smith "one Sorrell horse About fourteen hands high known by the name of Saml Martin's Sorrel: Which s^d Horse the s^d Smith purchased from the s^d Samuel Martin for the consideration of the Sum of One hundred pounds...."

The punctuation of this record is somewhat scant, but from the general context one gathers that Andrew Jackson paid one hundred pounds for the Horse, rather than that Thomas Smith paid this sum to Samuel Martin. At any rate "Samuel Martin's Sorrel" was valued at one hundred pounds—a rather goodly sum for young Attorney Jackson to be paying. Throughout his long life he continued to buy the best horses he could afford—they were a passion with him—and, unlike many devotees of the turf, he made money, rather than lost it, in his deals.

One of General Jackson's choice saddle horses was Duke, who is said to have been his favorite during the New Orleans campaign. If we credit the story of Uncle Alfred, the slave who for many years was his faithful bodyservant, he was mounted upon Duke on the day of victory. Mrs. Mary C. Dorris, in her *Preservation of the Hermitage*, quotes Uncle Alfred as saying:

> "General Jackson is ridin' Juke (Duke) dat day; he warn't ridin' Sam Patch, dat 'ar white horse standin' in de parlor.... He's ridin' Juke. An' Juke he dance Yankee-Doodle on three legs; and he dance it so plain dat de ban' struck up an' play 'Jackson, Jackson, yer's de man for me.'"

General Jackson, in a letter written to Mrs. Jackson during the Florida campaign of 1818, shows his affection for Duke.

> "I am advised there are a few red sticks (hostile Indians) west of Appelachecola, should this be true, I will have to disperse them, this done I shall commence my journey home. I am almost on foot, I almost despair of getting my favourite Old Duke home." (Bassett, *Correspondence of Andrew Jackson*, Vol. II.)

Uncle Alfred referred to the portrait in the Hermitage parlor, a work of the artist Earl, which shows General Jackson mounted on the white charger presented to him by the citizens of Philadelphia. He was a graceful and daring horseman and, like Washington and other great generals, had a passion for horses. He had also a country gentleman's interest in the breeding of blooded stock, and a sportsman's interest in their speed and bottom. There came a time, however, when he was forced to give up the turf—although never, for a moment, did he relinquish his interest in the breeding of fine horses at his Hermitage estate. The severe criticism of his horse-racing proclivities by his political enemies caused him, after his elevation to the Presidency, to discontinue training his colts for the track at the Hermitage.

*   *   *   *   *   *   *   *

But the log cabin days were ending. Fame came slowly, but certainly, to the humble dwelling in the midst of the fertile acres of the Hermitage. It was not sought by the master of the household, and it certainly was not welcomed by its mistress. It was impossible, however, for such a dynamic nature as Jackson's to avoid following an active and forceful course in the events of the period. He could no more stay at home when his presence was needed in the field than he could avoid taking a leader's place when he got into action. Each event in which he participated led him farther and farther from the simple life which he and his household had been leading, for with each success came promotions which gave the public greater and greater claims upon him.

The log cabin years, in spite of the struggles and tragedies sprinkled through them, were, on the whole, happy and eventful ones. The financial structure of the Hermitage household was strengthened, the public affairs of its master prospered, and his personal contacts with those who disagreed with him became less violent. Children had always been a part of the household. Rachel's brothers and sisters lived near by and their children, from babyhood to maturity, were her delight as well as General Jackson's. Added to these were the Butler children who, in the years of 1804 and 1805, became General Jackson's wards. In 1809, when twin boys were born to Severn Donelson's wife, the mother was quite frail, so Rachel carried one of her tiny nephews home with her and claimed him for her own. He was legally adopted and given the General's own name. After 1813 the Indian boy, Lincoya, orphaned at the Battle of Talluschatches, was taken into the friendly shelter of the Hermitage. A great favorite through the years was Andrew Jackson Donelson, who grew into a brilliant statesman under the General's fond care. Another valuable acquisition to the household was the young artist, Ralph E. W. Earl, who in 1818 married Jane Caffrey, one of Mrs. Jackson's numerous nieces.

Among the others who married Rachel's nieces were Abraham Green, of Natchez, who married Patsey Caffrey in January, 1801; General John Coffee, who married Mary Donelson in 1809; William Eastin, who married Mrs. Coffee's sister, Rachel Jackson Donelson, in the same year; and John C. McLemore, of Nashville. General Coffee's daughter, Mary, who as a young lady was a member of the Jackson household at the White House, married Andrew Jackson Hutchings, ward and grand-nephew of General Jackson. Through all the years the Jackson household knew the happy confusion which is common to large families—love, laughter, tears, and all of the things which go to make life full and interesting. No one reveled in these relationships more than the master, whose own near kin had been snatched from him by a series of tragic incidents of the Revolutionary War.

Mrs. Jackson had not been confined entirely, however, to her own family circles and the log Hermitage. After the victory at New Orleans she went south to join her husband. In the same year she accompanied him on a visit to Washington and to Virginia, and at all places she shared with him the honors showered upon him by an adoring populace. She accompanied him, too, when he went to Pensacola to assume the office of Governor of the Floridas, and from these trips returned laden with gifts and purchases which were somewhat out of place in the humble quarters to which they were brought. The time had come, obviously, for the building of a home more in keeping with the station of its master. Fortunately his financial status justified it. Otherwise the family would have undoubtedly remained in the log dwelling, for Andrew Jackson's good sense and determination to live within his means far outweighed any personal vanity. He was solicitous, however, of Mrs. Jackson's welfare, and was for her sake particularly interested in building a more suitable home.

The new Hermitage was built for Rachel, upon the spot which she selected. Major Lewis, Parton says, suggested it be built upon another more elevated site, but that General Jackson said to him:

> "No, Major, Mrs. Jackson chose this spot, and she shall have her wish. I am going to build this house for her. I don't expect to live in it myself."

General Jackson's health at this period was even worse than usual—and he was seldom well. The one thought uppermost in his mind when the new house was built was the comfort of the one person whom he loved above all other things in the world.

As houses go, the Hermitage of this period was by no means pretentious. It was a square-looking, home-like building, made of red bricks manufactured on the place by the slaves—spacious, comfortable, and liveable, but by no means elaborate. Many of the visitors who were thronging from all parts of the country to visit the "Hero of New Orleans" thought it a surprisingly simple abode for a man of such prominence. It was not, however, out of keeping with its local setting. Davidson County, according to the census of 1820, had a population of only 20,154 people. The section now known as Middle Tennessee was sparsely settled and still called "West Tennessee."

The period of transition from the log cabin to the ante-bellum mansion had begun, but most of the men who had fought their way to a financial security which justified the mansions still remembered their early days in pioneer cabins. Society was young and unexacting, and in the West they took Jeffersonian democracy literally. Andrew Jackson was himself the democrat of all democrats, but he had a poise and assurance which made him at home in all companies, and made all classes of people at ease in his presence. Neither his manner nor Mrs. Jackson's changed, however, with their removal to more handsome quarters. Both of them had long been known for their gracious hospitality and for a bearing which was at once simple and dignified.

Thomas Hart Benton, in writing of Mrs. Jackson, declared:

> "She had a faculty—a rare one—of retaining names and titles in a throng of visitors, addressing each one appropriately, and dispensing hospitality to all with a cordiality which enhanced its value. No bashful youth, or plain old man, whose modesty sat them down at the lower end of the table, could escape her cordial attentions any more than the titled gentleman on her right and left. Young persons were her delight, and she always had her house filled with them—clever young women and clever young men—all calling her affectionately 'Aunt Rachel.' I was young then, and was one of that number. I owe it to early recollections and to cherished convictions—in this last notice of the Hermitage—to bear this faithful testimony to the memory of its long mistress—the loved and honored wife of a great man." (From Benton's *Thirty Years' View*.)

It was Benton who gave to the world the picture of Andrew Jackson sitting before his fireside in the twilight with a child and its pet lamb on his knees.

THE STATELY AVENUE OF CEDARS AS IT APPEARS TODAY

When President Theodore Roosevelt visited the Hermitage in 1907 he alighted from his carriage at the entrance of the avenue and walked with bared head to the historic old mansion.

It was for gay groups such as those that Benton mentioned that the new Hermitage was built. In spite of the storm and stress the years were passing pleasantly with its mistress. Fame turned its spotlight upon the household, but the simple hospitality of the log cabin period was not abandoned. The spacious rooms of the new Hermitage rang with the laughter of a great bevy of nieces, of nephews, and neighbors' children. General Jackson's "military family," friends, and associates came from here, there, and everywhere, bringing with them members of their families and staying for weeks at a time. But the Hermitage acres were broad and fertile, the slaves were numerous and contented—and the mistress an excellent manager.

Years afterwards General Jackson wrote to young Andrew Jackson Hutchings (letter of April 18, 1833, Bassett, *Correspondence of Andrew Jackson*, Vol. V): "Recollect the industry of your dear aunt, and with what economy she watched over what I made, and how we waded thro' the vast expence of the mass of company we had. Nothing but her care and industry, with good economy could have saved me from ruin. If she had been extravagant the property would have vanished and poverty and want would have been our doom. Think of this before you attempt to select a wife."

The years in which this building was occupied were colorful and eventful ones in the Jackson saga. Unfortunately little is known of the actual details which attended its erection, the beginning of the garden, and other little intimate things concerning it. Even such a tireless student as the late John Spencer Bassett was not able to place exactly the time of its completion and occupation. Everything seems to indicate that it was started in 1818, about the close of General Jackson's Florida campaign, and that it was ready for occupancy, most likely, prior to June, 1819, the date of President Monroe's visit to Nashville and the Hermitage. The story is being pieced together, bit by bit, and it is gradually becoming complete.

A letter from Sir John Jackson, mentioned by Bassett, but secured in full from the manuscripts of the New York Public Library, by the Tennessee State Library, shows that in 1819 the Jacksons had secured the services of an English gardener. This letter reads:

"Philadelphia, April 30th, 1819.

"Major Genl A Jackson

"Dear General

"On the 26th Inst I wrote a few lines to you by William Frost a regular bred english Gardener who has been well recommended and from what I can judge from conversation with him am in hopes he will be found capable of whatever he undertakes—I engaged him for you as Gardener without any stipulation as to terms merely holding out that on his own capacity and industry his success and welfare depended—like others of his situation of life required an advance to bear his expense and had to give him 30 dollars on your account.

"I have seen a Nashville paper announcing your arrival and the congratulations of your Friends and fellow citizens testified by a Public dinner, it seems by the english Papers the english people are mad with the Citizens of N. York, this City and Baltimore for the respect shown you—with best respects to your Lady I remain with sincere respect and esteem, "Yours, "John Jackson."

In the same connection Bassett quotes a letter to William B. Lewis, which, though not dated, is placed sometime in 1819. It reads, in part:

"Sir, Mr. Wilson who was employed by Mr. Decker to paint my house has disappointed me, he was to have been here on the 15th he has not arrived. I will therefore now engage with the gentleman you spoke to me about, I have a Dearborn waggon in Town to day to bring up the tubes to convey water from my roof, and the ballance of the paint. will you have the goodness to see him for me. get him to go to Mr. Berkmans examine the bill of paints laid in, and if any wanting to add them, and to say to Mr. Berkman whether he prefers the Whitelead in oil or dry, and let it be brought up to day.

"I shall be down to day, to ride, but I am taken with an acute soreness in my left side, I cannot say pain, that is very troublesome when I bend, or is touched, perhaps it may with exercise disappear.

"I heard last evening that Mr. Rhea is in town I wish to see him, and if I can ride without great inconvenience I will be down for that purpose...."

The *Nashville Whig and Tennessee Advertiser*, of May 15, 1819, carried the announcement that the Hon. John Rhea was a candidate for Congress from the First District—it may have been that he was in Nashville at the time. The connection between his announcement and Jackson's letter is somewhat vague, but it may prove a small link in the chain which will eventually establish the date of the completion of this building.

Bassett mentions also a receipted bill for china and silver plate to the amount of $200, dated June 12, 1818, which, in 1922, was in the possession of Albert M. and Andrew Jackson, of Los Angeles. This, Jackson's letter about the paint, and Sir John's letter about the English gardener, indicate that the Hermitage household was to be conducted upon a more elaborate scale.

There is a strongly prevalent local tradition that the artist, R. E. W. Earl, laid out the Hermitage garden. It is quite possible that he worked with the English gardener in laying it out. He was established in Nashville as early as the latter part of the year 1817, for in the announcement of the Eighth of January Ball, 1818, some of his portraits were used in the decorations. The *Nashville Whig* of January 10, in describing the event, states:

> "The Ballroom was decorated with much taste, elegance and splendor. At the upper end of the room, were suspended three paintings, the portraits of Generals Jackson, Carroll and Coffee. Two of which, Generals Jackson and Coffee, were executed by a young artist now in this place, which, for boldness of design, accuracy of execution, judiciousness, and delicacy of shading would not lose in comparison with the finest paintings of modern times...."

An important visitor at the Hermitage that year was Isaac Shelby, "late governor of Kentucky," who stopped with the Jacksons while he and the General were preparing to go into the Chickasaw country to hold a treaty. Both men were popular, and their proposed mission was important enough to offer a sufficient incentive for an elaborate public dinner at the Nashville Inn.

At this dinner Col. Edward Ward, president, proposed the toast: "Isaac Shelby, late governor of Kentucky. The only governor in our Union who, during our late war, showed himself qualified for both the cabinet and the field."

John H. Eaton, Esq., vice president, proposed: "General Jackson, His military greatness commands our admiration—his private virtues our esteem."

Soon the generals and their suite were off for the Chickasaw country. They encountered some difficulty, for the *Nashville Whig* of October 10 reported that "but four chiefs attended on October 2nd"—they were alarmed at parting with any of their territory. On October 19, however, General Jackson wrote the following letter, announcing a successful conclusion of the mission:

> "Treaty Ground, October 19, 1818.
>
> "To the Editors of the Whig:
>
> "We have just closed a treaty with the Chickasaw Indians, for all their claims in the states of Tennessee and Kentucky, containing about seven millions of acres, of the best lands in the western country, and washed by the Tennessee, Ohio, and Mississippi Rivers, for at least three hundred and fifty miles: for an annuity of twenty thousand dollars for fifteen years.
>
> "I am respectfully, Your most obedient serv't, Andrew Jackson."

A month later, according to a paragraph in the Whig, the signing of the treaty was celebrated in Nashville:

> "A Tribute of Respect—A splendid Ball was given to General Jackson and staff, at the Nashville Inn, last Evening, in honor of the late Chickasaw Treaty."

Governor Shelby was not present, but he had found time to sit for the young artist at the Hermitage. General Jackson wrote him on November 24:

> "On the 20th the citizens of Nashville and its vicinity gave myself and Staff a Ball in commemoration of the late Chickasaw Treaty where I had the pleasure to see your Portrait suspended at the head of the assembly room and I was gratified to find that Mr. Earl had been so fortunate—for I can with truth say that there never came from the hands of an artist a better likeness...."

Earl married Jane Caffrey, niece of Mrs. Jackson, on May 19, 1818. The ceremony was performed by the Rev. William Hume. In less than a year the Reverend Mr. Hume was called upon to perform the sad duty of preaching her funeral sermon. The *Nashville Whig*, of March 13, 1819, carried the announcement:

> "The Rev. Mr. Hodge, assisted by the Rev. Mr. Hume, will preach the funeral sermon of the late Mrs. Earle, at the residence of Col. Stockely D. Hays on to-morrow."

Mrs. Jackson mothered and comforted the young man, and from that time, until his death in 1838, the Hermitage was his home. During the passing of the years he painted innumerable portraits of General and Mrs. Jackson, of the various kin, and of prominent visitors both at the Hermitage and the White House, where he was also a member of the household—so much a member, in fact, that he was dubbed "The King's Painter."

An intriguing, but forgotten, chapter in Earl's history was discovered by the writer a few years ago in the April 10th, 1822, issue of the *Nashville Whig*. A short article, headed quite casually, "Napoleon Buonaparte and Marshal Ney," announced: "Original portraits of these great men, taken by Mr. Earl, shortly after the return of Napoleon from the Island of Elba, were a few days since received and deposited by him in the Nashville Museum. Judging by his strikingly correct portraits of Gen. Jackson, of the President of the United States, of Shelby, of Haywood, and of a number of others, which likewise grace and ornament the Museum, we have no hesitation in believing them to be very exact likenesses...."

Where are these portraits of Napoleon and Marshal Ney, taken from life during the brief, but dramatic "one hundred days"?

One of the prominent visitors who sat for the young artist in his early days at the Hermitage was President Monroe, who visited Nashville and the Hermitage in June, 1819. The *Nashville Whig*, of Saturday, July 12, 1819, states:

> "The citizens having learned through the committee that the President had reached the residence of General Jackson, and that he would dine with them on Wednesday, last, set out on that day to meet and conduct him to this place. They met him four miles from town accompanied by Maj. Gen. Jackson and suite and Brevet Maj. Gen. Gaines. Three miles from town he was received by a large collection of the Tennessee Volunteers, armed and dressed as they were when they were in the several campaigns in which they had been engaged...."

The reception by this colorful procession which thronged the highway to the Hermitage to greet General Jackson and his distinguished guest was but the beginning of the festivities. A dinner followed at the Nashville Inn. President Monroe was entertained at the Nashville Female Academy on Thursday, June 10, and on the evening of that day the crowning event of his visit, a ball at the old Nashville Inn, took place.

"A numerous assemblage of elegance and beauty attended," said the editor of the *Nashville Whig*. "We have never seen more taste and beauty than was displayed in arranging the room, or a more numerous and brilliant assemblage of ladies. The arrangements were largely creditable to the managers. At the head of the room was a large transparency exhibiting an Eagle displayed and encircled in a ray of glory, bearing in his beak a transparent painting of our Chief Magistrate. Fronting at the lower end of the room, was suspended the portrait of Gov. Shelby of Kentucky. On the right side of the hall was a full length portrait of Maj. Gen. Jackson, with a distant view of the British encampment before New Orleans; fronting him were Genls. Coffee and Carroll. These inimitable paintings (with the exception of the transparency) were executed by our artist, Mr. Earl; and are highly honourable to the talents and profession aquirements of that gentleman. Over the paintings and around the room, were rich and beautiful festoons of evergreen and roses...."

A ray of glory—how the unknown artist of the transparency depicted it is a matter of conjecture, but the yellowed pages of the *Nashville Whig* bear testimony to its reality. It takes but small imagination to reconstruct the picture—men in handsome military uniforms, ladies in their gay-colored silks, dancing and conversing in the stately manner of the period, and paying due homage to the President of the United States and the Hero of New Orleans. At the Hermitage they found time, no doubt, to wander about in the moonlit, magnolia-scented grounds and to stroll along the paths of the new garden. Rachel, as she played the rôle of gracious, warm-hearted hostess, could not know that a long, lonely path, illuminated only by the cold rays of fame stretched before her adored husband, and that she, before a decade had passed, would rest under the friendly sod of her garden. Nor could President Monroe foretell the future of the distinguished soldier at his side. A great drama, of which the new Hermitage was to be the chief setting, was beginning.

It was not long until General Jackson was appointed governor of the Floridas, and he and Rachel moved their household temporarily to Pensacola.

"THE CHURCH WHERE JACKSON WORSHIPS"

A quaint old print of the church which General Jackson had built near the Hermitage in 1823-24 for the convenience of his pious wife and her neighbors.

"Gen. Jackson and family left town Saturday evening last in the Steam Boat Cumberland, on his way to Pensacola," says the *Nashville Whig* of April 18, 1821.

A little later it stated: "Gen. Jackson and family arrived at Natchez on April 21, on board the Steam Boat Rapide, having left Cumberland on account of some accident having happened to her machinery." The journey was completed in seven days, despite the accident! From Natchez, New Orleans, Blakely, Montpelier, and Mobile came echoes of a triumphant and leisurely progress. But even at that it was several weeks before the General and his suite were finally established in Pensacola—the Spanish governor was inclined to be a bit difficult about relinquishing his sway.

Rachel, however, did not like Pensacola. To her friend, Mrs. Eliza Kingsley, she wrote: "Believe me, this country has been greatly overrated.... One acre of our fine Tennessee land is worth a thousand.... The General, I believe, wants to get home again as much as I do...."

The General was not overly pleased with the situation and, as soon as he was able to settle certain little difficulties, he was determined to return to his beloved Hermitage. Marquis James, in his *Andrew Jackson, the Border Captain*, writes of this period:

"How peaceful the Hermitage! 'Our place looks like it had been abandoned for a season, But we have a cheirful fire for our friends, and a prospect of living at it for the ... ballance of our lives. I have sent on my resignation by Doctor Brunaugh.'

"It was over, this uncertain adventure into which Andrew Jackson had been drawn by an unreciprocated sense of loyalty to the President and a wish to help his young friends.... Rachel ... and Andrew undertook to make their home comfortable for the rest of their days. In the great hall stood seven cases of furniture and table silver purchased at New Orleans. However Rachel might deplore the wicked luxury of the complaisant Creole town there was no denying the comfort of good French beds. '1 Bedstead, of Mahogany, fluted, $100,' was for her own and Andrew's tall south chamber; likewise '1 Matress of fine ticking, $45, 1 moschette Bar of Muslin, $16, 1 Counterpane knotted, Marseilles, $24.' There was also a new sideboard and something to fill the decanters...."

There was dancing in the hallways in these days—dancing to the sound of a flute which "Old Hickory" himself may have played. Horace Holley, writing from Nashville on August 14, 1823, to his father, Luther Holley, Esq., in Salisbury, Connecticut (copy given to the author by the late Judge John H. De Witt), related:

"We have just returned from the Hermitage, ... The General called upon us in town on the evening of our arrival and he is one of the most hospitable men in the state. Mrs. Jackson is not a woman of cultivation, but has seen a great many people, has fine spirits, entertains well, and is benevolent. She is short in her person and quite fat. The General is lean and has been in ill health but is now invigorated and promises to live out his three-score and ten. He has built him a good brick house within the last two years and has finished it handsomely. Mary has taken three views of it in her sketch book. We looked at all the presents which have been made to the old warrior in honour of his military achievements and were gratified not a little.... The General has papers from most parts of the Union, and his study is loaded with piles of them. Considerable company was at his house every day, and our ladies danced every evening in the entry to the sound of the flute...." ("Mary" was Mary Austin Holley, author and cousin of Stephen Austin. Where are the sketches she made of The Hermitage?)

Andrew Jackson was content, Mr. James says, and "the measure of his contentment was in proportion to the sincerity of his resolution to exchange a brilliant career for a quiet one."

His peace was to be short-lived. On December 5, 1823, he took his seat in the Senate of the United States, to which he had been appointed by the Tennessee legislature. For six weary months he remained in Washington and Rachel, with her usual efficiency, kept the Hermitage household going. She was busy, for the little church which the General was building for her and her pious friends near the Hermitage was being completed. His letter, written in Washington, January 29, 1824 (which has been presented to the Ladies' Hermitage Association by the late Mr. Leland Hume, a descendant of the Rev. William Hume), states:

> "I am truly happy to hear that our church is about to be finished, and that pious good man Mr. Hume, is to dedicate it. If such a mans prayers cannot obtain a blessing upon the neighborhood, I would despair of the efficacy of prayer from any other...."

The church was completed and the General returned home—this time with the avowed intention of carrying Rachel with him when he returned to Washington the following autumn. In the meantime the presidential campaign of 1824 was in full swing, and the Marquis de Lafayette arrived with his son and suite to be the "nation's guest." On October 18 the distinguished Frenchman wrote to Jackson:

> "My dear General, With all the feelings of affectionate Gratitude I Have Received your kind and Highly Valued Letter: this is not However the first and greatest obligation that Binds me to general Jackson; Had you witnessed my anxiety when on a Sudden all Europe was pacified, and the flower of the British army were on their way to Louisiana, you would still Better judge what I felt of relief, joy, and pride, on Receiving the Glorious Account of your Victory: I Have long Anticipated the pleasure to take you by the Hand, and whatever Be your future movements I will Express in person my High Regard and Sincer friendship...." (Bassett, *Correspondence of Andrew Jackson*, Vol. III.)

Late autumn and winter took the Jacksons to Washington, where they put up at Gadsby's, which was also the quarters of the distinguished Lafayette. Here, on December 23, Mrs. Jackson wrote to her friend describing the meeting between the famous Frenchman and General Jackson.

> "We are boarding in the same house with the nation's guest, Lafayette. I am delighted with him.... When we first came to this house, the General said he would go and pay the Marquis the first visit. Both having the same desire, and at the same time, they met on the entry of the stairs. It was truly interesting. The emotion of revolutionary feeling was aroused in them both. At Charleston, General Jackson saw him on the field of battle; the one a boy of twelve, the Marquis, twenty-three. He wears a wig, and is a little inclined to corpulency. He is very healthy, eats hearty, goes to every party, and that is every night...." (From Parton, Vol. II.)

Rachel, too, for that matter was "a little inclined to corpulency." She did not attempt to attend all the parties, for Washington was unusually gay and her health was none too good. She paid calls, received large numbers of new acquaintances and old friends, and attended, of course, such important affairs as the eighth of January ball and Mrs. Monroe's drawing-room.

They stayed in Washington long enough to see General Jackson miss, by a hairbreadth, becoming President of the United States and to witness the pomp and ceremony of Mr. Adams' inauguration. They were home by the latter part of April, ready to take charge of their household again and to play host and hostess to Lafayette when he arrived in Nashville on the fourth of May. Never was there such a celebration!

Twenty-five thousand Tennesseans crowded into Nashville to welcome him. The military organizations of the state were out in full force, the ladies wore their finest dresses, and the streets were decorated with great triumphal arches of flowers. There were dinners and public programs of various types, but most important of all was the ball which was given for him in the Masonic Hall. Guild, in his *Old Times in Tennessee*, says:

> "The dance was opened by Gen. Jackson and the beautiful Miss McNairy. It was difficult to tell which was most to admire, the beauty and sylph-like grace of Miss McNairy, or the stately step and courtly manners of Gen. Jackson."

Mrs. Thomas Martin, whose narrative is quoted by Guild, in describing the ball said:

> "The old and the young were there, and the scene was one of beauty, fashion, and smiles. On a dais at one end of the hall were the guests and the old ladies—Gen. Lafayette with Mrs. Rachel Jackson, Gov. Carroll, with Mrs. Shelby, Gen. Jackson, with Mrs. Priestly and Mrs. Carroll, George W. Lafayette with Mrs. Stewart and Mrs. McNairy, and Mr. Shelby with Mrs. Minnick and myself...."

Stories of the ball are still recounted with delight in Nashville, and in many of the old families are fans, combs, dresses, and the gay little slippers of belles who "danced with Lafayette." But most interesting of all is the description of Lafayette's reception at the Hermitage, from the pen of his secretary, M. Levasseur:

> "At one o'clock we embarked with a numerous company to proceed to dine with General Jackson, whose residence is a few miles up the river. We there found numbers of ladies and farmers from the neighborhood, whom Mrs. Jackson had invited to partake of the entertainment she had prepared for General Lafayette. The first thing that struck me on arriving at the General's was the simplicity of his house. Still somewhat influenced by my European habits, I asked myself if this could really be the dwelling of the most popular man in the United States, of him whom the country proclaimed one of her most illustrious defenders; of him, finally, who by the will of the people was on the point of becoming her Chief Magistrate....

> "General Jackson," Levasseur continues, "successively showed us his garden and farm, which appeared to be well cultivated. We everywhere remarked the greatest order and most perfect neatness; and we might have believed ourselves on the property of one of the richest and most skillful German farmers, if, at every step, our eyes had not been afflicted by the sad spectacle of slavery. Everybody told us that General Jackson's slaves were treated with the greatest humanity...."

In this setting Rachel was at her best. She was now fifty-eight years old. Stout, kindly, motherly, and frankly growing old; but always the gracious hostess and always deeply interested in the gay doings of the young people who were drawn into the charmed circle of her hospitable household. Her garden had taken deeper root. Her house was more elegantly furnished and her acquaintance with the outside world had been greatly extended; but aside from the fact that she took her religion a little more solemnly and that she had been saddened by the malicious attacks made upon her, her nature had changed but little with the passing years. She never lost her love of people, her keen interest in things about her, nor her gentle sympathy.

The famous Frenchman and his entourage had hardly left when the Hermitage became the gathering place for a great corps of notables, who entered heart and soul into the campaign which placed its master in the President's chair and which completely vindicated its mistress. Never in the history of the nation has such a bitter, unscrupulous attack been waged against a candidate for public office; and never, under any circumstances, has an American woman received such shameful treatment at the hands of a political party. It is a page in history which is best overlooked.

However the storms raged on the outside, they did not change the happy atmosphere of the Hermitage. If the mistress suffered—as of course she did—she kept up a brave front for the General and the other members of her household. Henry A. Wise, later governor of Virginia, who was a guest at the Hermitage of this period, gives in his *Seven Decades of the Union*, an interesting picture of the house itself, as well as the social life which centered about it. This description is especially important, for it supplies the only known description of the interior of the brick house which was erected in 1819.

Wise had just been married to Anne Jennings, daughter of the Rev. Obadiah Jennings, Jackson's Presbyterian minister in Nashville, and the bride and groom, with their bridal party, had been invited to spend the honeymoon at the Hermitage.

> "We arrived at the Hermitage to dinner," Wise wrote, "and were shown to a bridal chamber magnificently furnished with articles which were the rich and costly presents of the city of New Orleans to its noble defender.
>
> "Had we not seen General Jackson before, we would have taken him for a visitor, not the host of the mansion. He greeted us cordially and bade us feel at home, but gave us to distinctly understand that he took no trouble to look after any but his lady guests; as for the gentlemen, there were the parlor, the dining-room, the library, the side-board and its refreshments; there were the servants, and, if anything was wanting, all that was necessary was to ring. He was as good as his word. He did not sit at the head of his table, but mingled with his guests, and always preferred a seat between two ladies, obviously seeking a chair between different ones at various times. He was very

easy and graceful in his attentions; free, and often playful, but always dignified and earnest in his conversation. He was quick to perceive every point of word or manner, was gracious in approval, but did not hesitate to dissent with courtesy when he differed. He obviously had a hidden vein of humor, loved aphorism, and could politely convey a sense of smart travesty. If put upon his mettle he was very positive, but gravely respectful. He conversed freely, and seemed to be absorbed in attention to what the ladies were saying; but if a word of note was uttered at any distance from him audibly, he caught it by a quick and pertinent comment, without losing or leaving the subject about which he was talking to another person—such was his ease of sociability, without levity or lightness of activity, and without being oracular or heavy in his remarks. He had a great power of attention and concentration, without being prying, curt, or brusque. Strong good sense and warm kindness of manner put every word of his pleasantly and pointedly in its right place.

ANDREW JACKSON, THE COUNTRY GENTLEMAN AT THE HERMITAGE

(Original presented to the Ladies' Hermitage Association in 1944 by Mrs. C. W. Frear, of Troy, N. Y., in memory of her husband.)

"To illustrate him in a scene: The Hermitage house was a solid, plain, substantial, commodious country mansion, built of brick, and two stories high. The front was south. You entered through a porch, a spacious hall, in which the stairs ascended, airy and well lighted. It contained four rooms on the lower floor, each entering the passage and each on either side opening into the one adjoining. The northwest room was the dining room, the southeast and southwest rooms were sitting rooms, and the northeast room had a door entering into the garden. The house was full of guests. There were visitors from all parts of the United States, numbering from twenty to fifty a day, constantly coming and going, all made welcome, and all well attended to.

"The cost of the coming Presidency was even then very great and burdensome; but the general showed no signs of impatience, and was alive and active in his attentions to all comers and goers. He affected no style, and put on no airs of greatness, but was plainly and simply, though impulsively, polite to all. Besides his own family he had his wife's relatives, Mr. Stokely and Andrew J. Donelson, around him every day, and his adopted son, Andrew Jackson, relieved him of all the minute attentions to guests.

"Henry Lee, of Virginia, was, we may say, resident for the time with him, as he was engaged in writing for his election some of the finest campaign papers ever penned in this country. One of Lee's fugitive pieces, on the death of an Indian youth, the son of a chief who was killed at the battle of the Horseshoe, whom the general had taken as a godson, an orphan of one of his victories, is a precious pearl of poetry in prose. (This refers to Lincoya and places his death about 1828. Where is Lee's article on his death? Both the Lee Foundation and the Ladies' Hermitage Association are interested in finding it.)... He was not as handsome as his half-brother, General Robert E. Lee....

"The first or second evening of our stay, Mr. Lee had drawn around him his usual crowd of listeners; but we were the more special guests of Mrs. Jackson. She was a descendant of Colonel Stokely of our native county, Accomack, Virginia, and we had often seen his old mansion, an old Hanoverian hip-roofed house, standing on the seaside, not far above Metompkin; and she had often heard her mother talk of the old Assawaman Church, not very far above Colonel Stokely's house, pulled down long before our day, endowed with its silver communion-service by our grandfather, George Douglas, Esq., of Assawaman. Thus she was not only a good Presbyterian too, but the groom was from the county of her ancestors, in Virginia, and could tell her something about the traditions she had heard from which she sprung...."

When there is added to Wise's description of the interior of the Hermitage of this period the view of the building and grounds included in Earl's 1831 portrait of General Jackson, the picture of the house as it was from 1819 to 1831 is complete. The *Nashville Republican* and *Tennessee Gazette*, on Thursday, August 25, 1831, repeated a criticism of this portrait which had appeared in the *Washington Globe*.

It reads, in part: "The artists of Boston announce it a 'first rate work,' and the intimate friends of the President consider it the most perfect likeness ever taken of him. It is not only recommended by this circumstance, but it is rendered doubly interesting as a sort of historical picture, in which the taste and talent of the designer is, in high degree manifested. The President stands alone in the solitude of the Hermitage. The scene is most accurately delineated. The house and surrounding grounds, although thrown somewhat in the distance, are identified to all acquainted with the spot, by its most striking features...."

To the west is seen a small square building which may have been used by General Jackson as an office. There is a tradition that it was Earl's studio and, since the artist was a member of the household in 1818 and 1819, it is more than likely true. There is a remote possibility that it was the kitchen, for the dining room, according to Wise's description, was "the northwest room," but it is more probable that the old kitchen was located near the present one, on the north side of the building. (Since 1933 a brick building, in the style of the period, has been erected on this foundation.) Traces of the foundation of this small building are still visible. It is important to observe further in this portrait which, in 1831, was accepted by the public and Nashville and in Washington as a historically accurate view of the Hermitage, there was still no evidence of the famous cedar-lined, guitar-shaped drive.

This portrait, which from an historical standpoint is probably the most important of the Jackson portraits, was presented to the Ladies' Hermitage Association in 1944 by Mrs. Charles W. Frear, of Troy, New York, in memory of her husband. For many years the Association did not know the location of the original, although it had long used a reproduction in its catalogue which, it appears, had been given to the organization about 1901 by McClure's Magazine. It is interesting that the acquisition of this famous portrait by the Ladies' Hermitage Association was perhaps due, in part, to the interest of a member of the artist Earl's family.

Mr. Ralph Earl Prime, Jr., of Yonkers and New York City, New York, writing to the author on October 8th, 1936, said:

> "I have borne in mind your interest in the 1831 portrait of Gen. Jackson with the Hermitage as a background, which was painted by Ralph E. W. Earl. I followed up the clue afforded by the article in the issue of McClure's Magazine in 1897, to which you called my attention, with the result that I have just received a letter, of which the following is a copy:—
>
> "'In reply to your letter of October 2, 1936, with reference to portrait of Andrew Jackson painted by Ralph E. W. Earl, will say the portrait was for many years in possession of the late Wm. H. Frear. It is now in my possession. The information you have in regard to the portrait is substantially correct to the best of my belief. Yours very truly, C. W. Frear.'
>
> "If he (Mr. Frear) could visit the Hermitage in person," Mr. Prime continued, "as I and some of my friends have done with so much satisfaction, and catch the spirit which actuates its custodians, I am sure that he would realize how appropriate it would be to restore the painting to its former setting as a gift to posterity, either presently or by his will...."

Happily, through Mrs. Frear's generosity, this treasure has been restored to *The Hermitage*, where it will remain through the years as a memorial to her husband.

This was Rachel Jackson's Hermitage—the Hermitage in which she entertained Monroe, Lafayette, and all that gay and distinguished company which, as stars in the great Jackson constellation, were destined, for a time, to dazzle the nation. And how many of them had known the kindly hospitality of the mistress of the Hermitage ... the quiet, studious, James K. Polk, who as "young Hickory" was to carry the Jackson banner again to the president's chair; Sam Houston, gay, lovable, and erratic, who was to be president of the Lone Star Republic; "Jeff" Davis, future president of the Confederate States of America; Thomas Hart Benton, destined to a powerful career in the United States Senate; John Eaton, John Coffee, William Carroll, and a score of others who shared the Jackson military and civil honors. All of them spent happy days under her roof and all of them, at some time during their career, took time to pay public tribute to her beloved memory.

As the year of 1828 drew to a close General Jackson's victory was assured. There was no personal elation in it for Rachel, however, just as there was no bitterness toward her persecutors during their most severe attacks upon her. Her reply when news of victory was brought to the Hermitage was: "For Mr. Jackson's sake, I am glad; for my own part, I never wished it. I had rather be a doorkeeper in the House of my Lord than to live in that palace in Washington."

She had always preferred the quiet of her own home and had resented the demands which fame made upon her husband. Her friends, though, were greatly elated for her sake, as well as for the General's. John H. Eaton, writing her from Washington, December 7, 1828, said:

> "The storm has now abated—the angry tempest has ceased to howl. A verdict by the American people has been pronounced of that high and grateful character, that for the honor of your husband, you cannot but look back upon the past as an idle fading vision carrying in it nothing substantial—nothing that should produce to you one moments feeling, or a moments pain. No man has ever met such a triumph before.... The Ladies from distance—from remote parts of the Union will be here—brought essentially and altogether on your account and to manifest to you their feelings and high regard: they will be present to welcome and congratulate you...." (Bassett, Vol. III p. 449.)

Nashville ladies were already busy doing their part to honor her— they were preparing a handsome wardrobe for her to carry to Washington with her, and the entire town was arranging a magnificent celebration for December 23, the anniversary of the night battle at New Orleans. Jackson leaders in Washington, Philadelphia, and other important places were preparing elaborate programs honoring the president-elect ... but on December 22 the rejoicing was turned into mourning. Rachel Jackson quietly slipped beyond the reach of cruel tongues.

Her illness came suddenly and unexpectedly a few days before the anticipated celebration. There are many versions of its origin. Some say that while in Nashville she was resting at the Nashville Inn and accidentally overheard some unpleasant remarks about her part in the past campaign. Others carry the story still farther and say that she wept and that, in returning to the Hermitage, she stopped her carriage at a creek to bathe her swollen eyes, and thus caught a cold. There could have been little shock connected with anything which she may have overheard, for she had been familiar with the attacks made on her throughout the past campaign. One thing which may be accepted as certain is that in some way she caught cold. Wise quotes a young Dr. Heiskell, of Winchester, Virginia, who was just starting as a physician in the neighborhood, and was the first doctor to reach her, as saying: "We learned that she had caught cold and pleuritic symptoms supervened upon her constitutional nervous affections. She was sitting smoking her corncob pipe when she caught her last malady...."

Wise further explains that "a pipe was prescribed by her physician for her phthisis, and she often rose in the night to smoke for relief." Whatever the explanation of the pipe may be, its only importance was its use in the caricatures used by her husband's opponents in the presidential campaign. She had long been subject to the bronchial trouble which was, undoubtedly, the chief cause of her death.

No words can describe the tragedy which stalked at the Hermitage during her illness. The General would not leave her side. The servants stood about in stricken silence, with the exception of old Hannah, who nursed her, and the few who were allowed to perform little duties to assist her. Friends and relatives gathered— and on the late afternoon of the twenty-second her condition seemed greatly improved. She had persuaded General Jackson to lie down on a sofa in the next room in order that he might be rested for the coming celebration—which, she insisted, he must attend. He obeyed and Mrs. Jackson was removed from her bed that it might be prepared for the night. As she sat in a chair, supported by the arms of the faithful Hannah, she suddenly uttered a cry and her head fell forward.... The General rushed to her and for a time, neither he nor his stricken household would believe that she was dead. At his command they placed her upon a table, the physician made an effort to bleed her, and they worked with her for hours before the desperate old man could understand that there was no hope. All night he remained by her side.

Early on the morning of the twenty-third the citizens of Nashville were informed of her death. It was ordered that on the following day, from one until two o'clock, the hour set for her funeral, that the church bells be tolled. The scene was rapidly changed from one of festivity to deep mourning, and on the next day the road was crowded with people on their way to the Hermitage to pay their last respects to a sainted woman. The Reverend William Hume preached her funeral sermon.

A gentleman from Philadelphia who was present wrote to a relative:

> "Such a scene I never wish to witness again. The poor old gentleman was supported to the grave by General Coffee and Major Rutledge. I never pitied any person more in my life. The road to the Hermitage was almost impassable, and an immense number of persons attended the funeral. The remains were interred in the lower part of the garden. I never before saw so much affliction among the servants in the death of a mistress. Some seemed completely stupified by the event; others wrung their hands and shrieked aloud. The woman who had waited on Mrs. Jackson had to be carried from the ground...."

The funeral service was, in fact, delayed because she had thrown herself upon her mistress' grave and refused to move. General Jackson would not allow her to be torn away by force, but waited patiently until her associates could persuade her to allow them to remove her.

So ended all thoughts of victory for Andrew Jackson. All that had made victory sweet, all that had made life worth while, had passed away. The only thing to which the broken old man looked forward was his return to their beloved Hermitage. His body, his mind, and his indomitable will he carried to Washington—but his heart he left buried with Rachel in their garden.

Although for a time after her death Rachel Jackson's Hermitage—the building as it appeared from 1819 to 1831—remained unchanged, the period was, to all intents and purposes, ended. The household and its followers centered about the White House, and the lonely resting place of its mistress was left to the tender care of relatives and the slaves whose grief was still inconsolable.

General Coffee, R. E. W. Earl, Andrew Jackson Donelson and his wife, Emily, who was for a time mistress of the White House; Andrew Jackson, Jr., and later his bride, Sarah York Jackson; Major Lewis, and others formed a part of the household. Some of the time three Marys—Mary Coffee, Mary McLemore, and Mary Eastin—daughters of Rachel's nieces, added gayety to the Washington household. Mary Eastin was married in the White House to Lucius Polk, and Mary Coffee married General Jackson's ward, Andrew Jackson Hutchings.

A new phase in the history of the Hermitage began in 1831. Andrew Jackson, Jr., married the beautiful and cultured Miss Sarah York, of Philadelphia, on November 24, 1831. Some interest in the future began to live in the heart of Andrew Jackson. Since his wife's death he had contemplated his son's marriage with more than ordinary concern.

"It is," he wrote to a friend in May, 1829, "the only hope by which I look to a continuation of my name...."

It proved to be more than that for it was the beginning of a beautiful relationship destined to last from the time he welcomed Sarah York Jackson, as a bride, to the White House, until she stood at his deathbed at the Hermitage in 1845. The President, because of pressing duties and ill health, had not been able to make the journey to Philadelphia to attend the wedding, but he sent Col. Earl with a cluster of pearls for the bride. It was in the form of a ring, and there was a lock of his hair on the under side of the setting. With it he sent the message that from his son's description of her he thought "pearls the most fitting gift, as emblematic of the purity of her character and the beauty of her face." (From the notebook of Mrs. Rachel Jackson Lawrence—State Library.)

The wedding took place at the home of Mrs. Samuel Wetherill, Sarah York's sister, who lived on Chestnut Street, in Philadelphia. Mrs. Jackson, Mrs. Wetherill, and another sister, Mrs. Adams, were left orphans in early childhood, and, at the request of their dying father, were cared for and educated at Mrs. Malland's boarding school. They were well-bred, charming, and well connected. Andrew Jackson himself—and he was a noted matchmaker—could not have made a better choice for the future mistress of the Hermitage.

Before Andrew Jackson, Jr., brought his bride to the red brick mansion in Tennessee, extensive remodeling was done. This period in the history of the Hermitage had been completely overlooked until a letter in the Hermitage collection was recently brought to light. This letter (Published for the first time in the 1933 edition of the present work) which is quoted in full, gives complete data on the remodeling of the Hermitage in 1831, as well as the building of the tomb in the garden. It reads:

"Nashville, December 6, 1831.

"Dear sir: I have the satisfaction to inform you that the additions and improvements to the Hermitage are compleated. I have in addition to the improvements, as exhibited on the plan furnished you a neat and appropriate Portico on the back side of the center building, which adds very much to the comfort & convenience of your dwelling.

"The Hermitage as improved presents a front of 104 feet, the wings project 9 feet in front the center building and are connected by a colonnade of the same breadth. The colonnade consists of 10 lofty columns of the Doric order the entablature is carried through the whole line of the front, and has wreaths of laurel leaves in the frieze, on the cornice is a blocking corse that support an appropriate balustrade. The upper story consists of a Portico surmounted by a pediment which breaks the monotony of the composition in a very satisfactory manner.

"The material employed in the emprovements are all of the best quality the neighborhood affords, the colonnade is covered with the best copper the sheets weighing from 12 to 14 lbs. each sheet, and the gutters that convey the water from front to back are also of copper. The wing buildings and Porticos are roofed with good ceader shingles. The old Kitchen is removed and the matereals employed in the erection of a large and comodeus smoke house which is placed on a line with the new kitchen. The internal arrangements are almost to my mind. The dining room is large and will dine 100 persons at one time comfortable. The wing at the East end contains the library a large and comodeous room and overseer room, and a covered way that protects the three doors leading to the library the overseer room and to the back parlor.

"In the progress of the emprovements I adhered as closely to the plan furnished you as circumstances would admit. The only alteration I have made is in adding 2 feet to the length of the Kitchen, and 20 feet to the length of the East wing. The latter was done at the request and with the advice of Gen. Coffee which additions I hope will meet with your approbation.

"The following is the amount that has been expended independent of what has been done by your one (own) hands—

Cash	to stone-cutters, mason & bricklayers	491.00
"	to carpenters and joiners	678.00
"	to painters and glazers	187.00
"	plasterers	168.00
"	copper smith and tinner	350.00
"	Lumber and shingles	468.50
"	Hardware glass &c.	110.00
"	Lurners (?) bill	25.00
"	Halling lumber from Nashville	11.00
		$2488.50

"You will perceive by this amount notwithstanding the several additions, the back Portico, and many additional expenses incident to such emprovements I have been able to effect it with a less sume than the original estimate which to me is a source of gratulation without respect to any hope of pecuniary emolument. I must entreat you to believe that no such sordid matire entered into my views. To merit your approbation has been my ambition, to succeed in obtaining it is my best reward—I have received in addition to the fifteen hundred Dollars the amount of your chieck, Five hundred dollars from Mr. Josiah Nicholl, making two thousand dollars, leiving a ballance of Four hundred and eighty-eight Dollars.

"On receipt of your letter of the 18th August for which I return you my thanks for the expressions of kindness it contains, I employed an expereanced stone-cutter in whome I have entire confidence who is progressing with the Temple & Monument it will be composed intire of stone. The massivenes of the parts of the Grecian Doric order require a material of great strength such as the white stone of this neighborhood and when this can be obtained it must always be a subject of regret that recourse should be had to any imitation of it however exact:

but I found it impossible to get ceader timber large enough to be wrought into the forms required. The principle cost of this substantial and highly ornamental emprovement consists of the hire of stone cutters, and the purchase of copper for the covering of the doom. I expect in the progress of this work to have the ade of your one hands & teems in quarry & halling the stone, which will enable me to bestoe an additional quantity of labor on the building, in order that it may fully meet publick expectation. I am anxious to have it finished as soon in the spring as possible, in as much as I will be necessary detained hear to direct the operation of the workmen in order that it may be in conformity to the plan furnished you.

"I have made a drawing of the Hermitage as emproved, which is in the hands of an experanced engraver, it will make a splendid picture and as soon as it is finished I will send you a copy which will give you a better idea of the building than any written discription I can give—my best respects to your son— Mrs. M joins with me in tendering you, not our complements, but our kindest & best wishes,

"I am your most obldge D Morrison."

Notes in Andrew Jackson's own hand on the back of the letter read: "Mr. Morrison rec'd & answered. A bill for $300 inclosed to Mr. Morrison or Josiah Nichol. A. J. To be preserved. A. J."

The picture which Mr. Morrison mentioned has been preserved. It appears on Ayres' Map of Nashville, which was published in 1832. An announcement of the plans for this map appeared in the *Nashville Republican* and *State Gazette*, of December 6, 1831— strangely enough, the exact date of Mr. Morrison's letter. This notice reads:

"Map of Nashville—Sketches of the embellishments which are to be attached to this work have been politely submitted to our inspection. They consist of three different views of the City— one from the bank of the Cumberland near the ruins of the Old Steam Mill; another from a hill on the South near the residence of Dr. Overton, and the third from a commanding height about two miles to the North—the Penitentiary from an iminence in front, with its beautiful back-ground scenery of hill and wood and cultivated field—a portion of College Street including Yeatman and Woods' Bank—the U.S. Branch Bank—a group consisting of the Court House, Inn and Hotel—a part of the Public Square including the upper end of the Market House—the University and background—the Presbyterian, the Baptist, and the Episcopal churches—the Female Academy and other buildings in the neighborhood. To these is added a view of the Hermitage in its present newly finished state, than which there is not to be found west of the Allegany a more beautiful and splendid private residence."

A comparison of the engraving on Ayres' map with Mr. Morrison's letter proves the authenticity of the picture. There are ten columns instead of the six stately ones of the present, and the exterior of the building corresponds in other details with his description. The tomb, for the artist's convenience, more than likely, is placed nearer the house than it is in reality.

Andrew Jackson Baker, present caretaker of the Hermitage, who has made a careful study of the building, points out a number of irregularities in the doors of the east wing which are due, undoubtedly, to the remodeling. The brick walls themselves show where the east wing was added and where there was once a little roof or porch extending over the entrance to the cellar. The kitchen and smoke-house, as Morrison's letter states, are on line with each other.

The handsome remodeled Hermitage which was Mr. Morrison's and Nashville's pride was destined, however, to a career of short duration. In October, 1834, it caught fire and was, with the exception of the dining-room wing and its sturdy brick walls, destroyed. The catastrophe is described in the *Nashville Republican* of October 14, 1834, as follows:

> "The Hermitage Burnt—Yesterday evening about 4 o'clock the roof of the Hermitage was discovered to be on fire, and all attempts to arrest the progress of the flames proving unavailing, the entire edifice, with the exception of the room attached to the northern end and used as a dining room, was in a few hours consumed. The valuable furniture in the lower story was fortunately saved, though much broken and otherwise injured in getting it out. That in the second story was, we understand, chiefly destroyed. The fire is supposed to have been communicated to the roof by the falling of a spark from one of the chimneys, and there being a breeze from the northwest, the progress of the flames was proportionably rapid. The numerous and valuable private papers of the President were probably all preserved.

> "We need not add that the event has occasioned to this community deep and universal regret."

Letters from Bassett's *Correspondence of Andrew Jackson*, give further details of the fire. On October 14, 1834, Col. Robert Armstrong, Nashville's postmaster, wrote:

> "My dear Genl. Your son and Majr. Donelson have both written you the perticulars of the unfortunate burning of the Hermitage House. We heard the news Last evening but not the extent of the Damage. I sent One of the Young men Out of the Office up After supper who returned by Sun up this morning. I learned from Majr. D. and the Young man I sent up that all the furniture and valuables with the papers, letter Books, etc., have been with the exception of some furniture upstairs (the Wardrobe and Large bedstead) saved. Some few things were singed in getting out but on the whol I expect everything was done that could be done and I have no doubt it was purely accidental. The House can be rebuilt on the Old Site for $2,000 or 2,500. The dineing room wing is but Little injured. I will go up this evening to see your Son and also Mr. Rife, the Carpenter doing Majr. D. work, and the one who built my House and will write you in a day or two. I will see what will be his estimate and Austins for its Complete Rebuilding and inform you...."

Stockley Donelson, General Jackson's nephew, wrote on the same day, giving details of the fire.

> "A fire was kindled in the old dining room," he stated, "and the chimney caught on fire, which not being observed immediately, and the wind being from the North west, the fire was communicated to the roof. The flame however had not spread very far before it was discovered by Squire and Charles and the alarm given. Cousin Sarah at this moment was in the house having just returned from a short ride and Andrew was in the field, but a short distance from the House, The fire was soon discovered by Wm. Donelson hands who were working near at hand, by A. J. Donelson work men and hands, as well as by your own hands. They were all on the ground before the roof fell in, etc. Mr Rife by his own exertions succeeded in getting on the dining Room roof and extinguishing the flames, etc. Others were employed in getting out the furniture, etc., which was nearly all saved, except some bedsteads up stairs.... Cousin Sarah acted with firmness and gave every necessary

direction to save the furniture, and Her and Andrew though much Hurt, I am happy to add bear the misfortune with fortitude.

PARLORS AT THE HERMITAGE

Below: THE FRONT HALL

Showing the stairway and the historic Telemachus wall paper.

"*The walls of the House being originally well built are not much damaged.* The workmen Austin, Rife, etc say there will be no difficulty in rebuilding, etc. Some of the petition walls and arches over the windows, and some other repairing of the walls all of which Mr. Austin can furnish brick to do by deferring the building of some of Maj Donelson back buildings.... Andrew requested me to say to you that he would move to the Baldwin place, and will start 3 or 4 whip saws tomorrow, and will get ready to cover it immediately, which is entirely practicable...."

Col. Armstrong, after his promised visit, wrote: "The dineing room Wing is but Little injured and I view it this way that you have now the Stone and Brick-work of your House done, and one Wing Complete, and that 2500$ will Compleate the main house and the other office Wing. The Kitchen and out Houses are all safe."

Like most estimates, Col. Armstrong's proved to be far lower than the final cost. The first estimate made by Joseph Rieff and William C. Hume amounted to $3,950. Added to this was $239 "for Extra work done upon change of Plan;" $186, "for work done on West wing and New Kitchen finding everything;" and $750 "for the full length two story Porch added finding every thing;" making a grand total of $5,125.

Among the interesting items included in the first estimate were: "1 Circular stair case 2 storys high, $260; first story of front poarch with 6 collums etc, $256; second story of ditto, $75; one back Portico, $40...." (Complete details of the rebuilding are found in Bassett's *Correspondence of Andrew Jackson*, Vol. V.)

A new house called, of course, for new furnishings. Sarah York with the adored little Rachel, born November 1, 1832, and her infant brother, Andrew, went on to visit the General at the White House. On this visit Sarah went on to Philadelphia to visit her own kin and while there made selections for the paper and the furnishings of the Hermitage.

One of the hitherto unpublished letters of the Hermitage collection, written at Washington April 14, 1835, by General Jackson, shows his interest in the furnishings, as well as his tender solicitude for Sarah York and the children:

"My dear Sarah: When you get a little rested from your journey make enquiry about the bedsteads and let me know at what the eight can be procured, of good plain mahogany.... I shall be anxious to hear from you, how my dear little Rachel is, as well as yourself and Andrew—I have great solicitude about my dear little Rachel. Keep the dear little ones for me—present me kindly to Mr. & Mrs. Wetherall and accept a father's prayers for your health and happiness. We all salute thee kindly. Andrew Jackson."

Sarah busied herself with shopping and soon she had purchased a splendid new outfit for the Hermitage. The bill, dated January 2, 1836 (*Correspondence of Andrew Jackson*, Vol. V.) included:

> 6 Mahogany Bedsteads, including the packing at 40, $240; 24 Fancy Chairs cain seat rich blue and gold at 2.50, $60; 4 Curtins, Crimson Silk lined with white Silk and full mounted at 75, $300; box $1, $301; 7 pair Tongs and Shovel polished steel pairs at 4.50, $31.50; 1 pair Do large, $75.50; 1 pair Chamber Candlesticks plated, $6; 1 Brass Fender, best, $13, box $1, $14; 1 Wardrobe Black and ornamented $50; 2 Wash Stands marble tops at $18, $36; 2 Do small at $5; $10; 2 large size Bureaus at $30, $60; 2 Center Tables at $30, $60; 8 Packing Boxes, $16.50; 5 Wire Fenders with Knobs, at $4.50, $22.50; 1 Nurcery Fender, $6.50; Box, $1.75; 2 pair Brass Andirons at $6, $12; 1 pair Brass Andirons, $6.50; 2 pairs Brass Andirons at $7, $14; 3 Setts of fine paper hanging Views Telemechus at $40, $120; 150 yards Super Nankeen Matting at .50, $75; 20 Yards Brussels 4-4 Stair Carpeting Crimson Damask Center with net Border at $2.87½, $57.50; 1 mahogany Bedstead packed, $40; 1 Mahogany Bedstead packed very fine, $60; 1 Blind large Size, $10; 1 pair Blinds to match, $10; 1 doz. 40 inch Stair rods $6.50; Box, $1.75. The grand total, including insurance on the shipments made on the boats, Bonnaffe, Mile, and Jno Sergeant, amounted to $1,364.50.

There was trouble about the wall paper, and again General Jackson's friend, Col. Armstrong, came to the rescue. He wrote, on May 27, 1836 (Bassett's *Correspondence*, Vol. V.):

> "Dear Genl. I send you inclosed a note addressed to me by the Mess. Yeateman after a conversation I had with them this morning. They have always been ready and willing to do all in their power to get back the paper from those who purchased it. When I call'd on Campbell I expected to get the paper, that night he cut it and put it on the Walls.
>
> "Williams is not at home. I saw Shelly who will do nothing in it, he is not disposed to restore it. Williams *dare* not, as his wife

claims it, so I call'd on the Mess. Yeateman and stated the facts who willingly proposed to purchase another set...."

There has long been a tradition in Nashville that the old Campbell house, not far from town, on the Lebanon Pike, had paper like that in the Hermitage hall, but it was, evidently, destroyed when the walls were scraped and re-papered. Further details concerning the determined woman who kept the paper have not, at the present writing, come to light.

A bill dated May 30, 1836, shows that Jackson's merchant and personal friend, Henry Toland, of Philadelphia, arranged for another shipment of paper. This bill includes the items: "3 Views of Telemachus at $29, $87; 7 ps Pannell Paper, at $2.50, $17.50; 7 ps. Bordering, at $3.00; $21; 4 ps. Plain Blue, at .75, $3." A box cost fifty cents and five per cent was deducted because of the cash payment, making the final amount $122.60. The bill is marked "Received payment fr H Toland, October 25th 1836. Robert Golder, per Jas. Cameron Golder."

Nancy McClelland, in her monumental work, *Historic Wall-Papers*, (Lippincott Company, Philadelphia, 1924) states that "the complete set consisted of 25 strips in colours, and the scenes are constructed on the account of the adventures of Telamachus." It was manufactured in Paris by Dufour about 1825 and, though rare, was not an exclusive pattern. It is still found on the walls of certain historic homes and in a few private and public collections.

According to the late Mrs. Rachel Jackson Lawrence, daughter of Sarah York and Andrew Jackson, Jr., the Telemachus paper now on the walls of *The Hermitage* hallway is the third set of its kind purchased by General Jackson. The first, she declared, was put on the walls at the time of the remodelling in 1831 and was burned in the fire of 1834. The second was the one acquired by Mrs. Campbell and the third, which, like the others, is the work of Dufour, was placed on the walls some time after it was ordered in the late spring of 1836.

Sarah York selected papers for the Hermitage, but, as his letter of April 14, 1835, (Hermitage MSS. Collection) shows, President Jackson took a personal interest in the Telemachus paper.

"I rec' a note from Mr. Toland," he wrote, "after you left us, informing that Mr. South had forwarded the order to Paris for the Telamucus and the other would be detained until you arrived and made the selection for those rooms not selected for. As soon as you can attend to this and have the selection made and the paper shipped for New Orleans so that it may get up to Nashville before the Steam boats stop running. I have written Mr. Toland on this subject...."

Eighteen packages of furniture for the Hermitage were lost when the steamer *John Randolph* was burned at Nashville, May 16, 1836, but it is evident that they were replaced as quickly as possible. There was always, however, the delay of waiting for sufficiently high water, in addition to the long, tedious journey around the coast to New Orleans and up the Mississippi, Ohio and Cumberland to Nashville.

Another large bill of furnishings for the Hermitage was purchased of Barry and Krickbaum, of Philadelphia, in February, 1837. It included 1 Large Wardrobe, $75; 2 dressing Bureaus to match, $110; 2 Wardrobes, french pattern, $120; 1 Eliptic front Bureau, $5; 1 Secy and Bookcase complete, $50; 2 pier tables, marble tops, $120; 1 Work table Elegantly fitted up, $50; 1 Work Stand, marble tray top, $5; 2 Work Stands, marble tray top, $50; 1 Marble Slab, $10. Total $665.

About the same time a long list of smaller furnishings amounting to $481.93 was bought of Lewis Veron and Company, Philadelphia. There were fenders, and irons, screens and such, things. Among them were "2 Pair french And Irons $70; 1 Gallérie for fire place, $55; 1 Clock Shade and Stand, very large, $17; 1 Plated Egg Boiler, $19; and one Silver Mounted Butter Tub, $12." (The list is given in full in Bassett's *Correspondence*, Vol. V.)

The new furnishings, with such as were left from the fire, were assembled in a harmonious whole toward the end of General Jackson's second term as President. Sarah York, after her arrival at the Hermitage in 1832 had bought carpets, linens, and various necessities. General Jackson had written his son at this time:

> "Sarah writes me about a Carpet for the dining room and some table linnen and common furniture for the Table. There were abundant supply. of table linnen, etc. etc. when we left the Hermitage, but I suppose it must have gone the same way as the sheets. I have said in my letter to Sarah inclosed that a carpet must be bought for the dining room. There is always a supply of the carpets made by the Shakers, to be had at Mr. Nichols, and she must buy such furniture as the House wants,

having an eye to proper economy. This you will have done agreeable to her directions. I have named domestic carpet, as it will be cheaper and better than an oil cloth or matt...."

Again he wrote: "View those East India matts or carpeting and see whether these recommended by Mr. Toland will answer better for the passage than oil cloth, and whether Sarah would prefer these to common carpets for the bedrooms...."

After all the delays and the characteristic confusion of moving the furnishings—old and new—were at last arranged. A weary old man—ill and hemorrhaging heavily from the lungs—turned his face eagerly to the spot which, in all the world, he loved best. To Nicholas P. Trist he wrote on March 2, 1837, "Your letter ... found me confined to my room, indeed, I might say to my bed, and I have been only four times down stairs since the 15th of Novb. last, altho I have been obliged to labour incessantly.... Tomorrow ends my official carier forever, on the 4th I hope to be able to go to the capitol to witness the glorious scene of Mr. Van Buren, once rejected by the Senate, sworn into office...."

Late in December, 1936, he had written Andrew Jackson Donelson, a letter of condolence—the spirited Emily, whom he loved deeply, but whom he, in high dudgeon, had sent home because she refused to receive the much-discussed Peggy O'Neal Timberlake Eaton, had succumbed to a lung trouble similar to that from which he was suffering.

> "I have this moment recd. the sad and melancholy intelligence that our Dear Emily is no more.... I have no language in which I can express my grief.... My health is slowly returning, and my strength improving slowly...."

THE GARDEN AND THE TOMB

Upon the tomb is carved General Jackson's immortal tribute to his wife: "Her face was fair, her person pleasing, her temper amiable, her heart kind; she delighted in relieving the wants of her fellow creatures, and cultivated that divine pleasure by the most liberal and unpretending methods; to the poor she was a benefactor; to the rich an example; to the wretched a comforter; to the prosperous an ornament; her piety went hand in hand with her benevolence, and she thanked her creator for being permitted to do good. A being so gentle and so virtuous slander might wound, but could not dishonor. Even Death, when he bore her from the arms of her husband, could but transport her to the bosom of her God."

The rest, sunlight, and pleasant atmosphere of the Hermitage were destined, however, to work a great improvement. His wiry, long-suffering body was to recover sufficiently for him to spend eight years in his new home before he was laid to rest in the garden beside the beloved Rachel. During these years his young men, under his wise guidance, had a tremendous influence in the nation—and in 1845, James K. Polk, who had openly conducted his campaign as "Young Hickory," the legitimate political heir of the "sage of the Hermitage," was inaugurated.

Andrew Jackson and his family, after Van Buren's inauguration, made a triumphant progress southward and, on March 25, 1837, reached the Hermitage. To Martin Van Buren he wrote on March 30: "I reached home ... with a very bad cough, increased by a cold taken on board the Steam Boat.... I hope rest in due time may restore my health so as be enabled to amuse myself in riding over my farm and visiting my neighbors...."

But however interested he was in his farm and his neighbors he took time to write his successor and protégé several pages of very sound advice on state affairs:

> "Fearlessly pursue your principles avowed, and the people will sustain you against all apostates, ambitious, and designing men ..." and take care of "the safety of the deposit Banks of the West, and south...."

From that time onward the Hermitage was prominent in the eyes of the nation. The younger statesmen paid visits to "the sage of the Hermitage" as the ancients consulted oracles—and the masses continued to worship the "Hero of New Orleans."

His domestic life flowed easily and pleasantly under the skilled and tactful direction of his daughter, Sarah. The adored little Rachel dogged his footsteps, rode with him, and, with her bright prattle, enlivened his days. Mrs. Marion Adams, Sarah's older sister, now widowed, made her home at the Hermitage, and Rachel's relatives came from their neighboring estates to pay respects to their beloved kinsman. Never was a lonely old man surrounded with greater affection or more kindly care.

But what of the outward appearance of the Hermitage of this period? There is every indication that the cedars along the driveway were set out at this time. A drawing of the Hermitage dated 1856 indicates that the cedars were still quite young at that time, and a statement of Parton, based on his visit to Nashville prior to the publication of his *Life of Andrew Jackson* in 1859, further corroborates it and gives, as well, an interesting picture of the appearance which the Hermitage finally assumed after its series of changes. He wrote:

> "Now we leave the turnpike and turn into a private road, straight, narrow, a quarter of a mile long, the land on both sides dead level. We come to a low iron gate in a white wooden frame, which admits us to an avenue of young cedars, ending in a grove, through which a guitar-shaped lawn is visible.... We alight, at length, on the stone steps of the piazza, and the Hermitage is before us.... A two-story brick house, with a double piazza both in front and in the rear; the piazza wooden and painted white supported by thick grooved pillars of the

same material and color. The floors of the lower piazza are of stone, and each terminates in a wing of the house...."

A familiar and cherished picture to Tennesseans, and to many thousands of Americans who have journeyed the same road to pay tribute to the memory of Andrew Jackson. Parton, like the Frenchmen with Lafayette, was struck by the simplicity of the Hermitage, but he was much impressed with the fertility of the land and the natural beauty of the estate. Like the Frenchmen, he, too, was much concerned with the "sad spectacle" of slavery, but he was convinced that the Jackson slaves had an unusually happy lot.

The best-known authority on the laying out of the cedar drive is the narrative of Mrs. Rachel Jackson Lawrence ("little Rachel") which appears in the second volume of the late S. G. Heiskell's *Andrew Jackson and Early Tennessee History*. Mr. Heiskell was not only an eminent lawyer, but he was a careful and painstaking historian. He quotes Mrs. Lawrence as saying:

> "Colonel Earle assisted in laying off the grounds, the front yard, at the Hermitage. My mother drew the plan, and Colonel Earle superintended the laying off, and the planting of all those cedars you can see there. He also laid off the center of the Hermitage garden. I think it was exposure to the sun, after being so closely confined in his studio, that resulted in his death. He came in, I remember, and sat down at the dinner table, and said he did not feel very well, thought he had something like a chill.... When supper time came, he was still feeling very badly.... About daylight he died with a congestive chill."

Earl's death was mentioned in General Jackson's letters of September, 1838. "His death," he wrote, "is a great bereavement to me ... he was my friend and constant companion...."

Mrs. Lawrence's statement does not definitely place the laying out of the flower beds in the center of the garden. It is possible that, in those lonely days after his young wife's death in 1819, he worked with Rachel Jackson in the garden of her new home. Frost, the English gardener may have worked with them. At any rate, the garden grew as the estate developed and, through the twenty years of his residence at the Hermitage, it must have delighted the beauty-loving soul of the artist.

But what suggested the guitar as a model for the drive? There is a tradition that General Jackson selected it because Rachel played the guitar—certainly, even at Hunter's Hill, she played a harpsichord, and often accompanied the General when he played upon his flute. There is definite proof that Sarah York had a guitar, for General Jackson, in a letter written in Washington, April 12, 1832, said: "Your cousin Saml. J. Hays has agreed to take the Dog—will rest at Rockville with you tonight. He takes on Sarah's Gator (guitar)—you must direct him where to leave it...."

Somewhere the connection between music and the cedars was seen by a mind poetic enough to look forward to a day when they would grow into a massive instrument upon which the pleasant winds might play. Perhaps "Old Hickory" himself conceived the idea—at any rate he approved it, or the drive would not have been planted. It is enough to know that in planting the trees he connected them with the music of at least one—perhaps two—mistresses of the Hermitage.

General Jackson was interested, too, in the willows which he had planted by Mrs. Jackson's tomb and in the flowers she had loved. In a letter written to Andrew Jackson, Jr., on August 20, 1829, he expresses deep concern for the care of her grave in the garden:

> "In your letter although you have informed me of your visit to your dear mother's tomb, still you have not informed me of its situation, and whether the weeping that we planted around it are growing, or whether the flowers reared by her industrious and beloved hands, have been set around the grave as I requested. My D'r son, inform me on this subject, you know it is the one dearest to my heart, and her memory will remain fresh there as long as life lasts...."

"As long as life lasts...." Each evening at sunset a failing old man turned his footsteps toward the garden. The chattering little girl who held his hand paused at the gate and watched in silence while he made his way slowly down the garden paths to the white stone temple in the lower end of the garden.

> "No one ever went to the tomb with him," Mrs. Lawrence told Mr. Heiskell. "I always went to the gate, and saw him in, but I realized he was going to the tomb. He would stay there a half hour, I suppose, then return. He did this as long as he was able to walk."

It was not long to wait. Louis Philippe sent the artist Healy to paint his portrait, and Sam Houston was hastening from Texas that his fast-failing friend might lay his hands on his young son's head in blessing. The portrait was finished three days before the old General's death, but Sam Houston reached the Hermitage just a few hours too late.

The end came quietly and peacefully on June 8, 1845, and two days later Andrew Jackson was laid to rest beside his beloved Rachel. Their mortal remains have rested peacefully in the earth they loved these many years, while the changing seasons have brought their fleeting beauty to the garden—but who shall say that their story has not become immortal?

ADDITIONAL NOTES

(Plans for this volume were made during Mrs. E. A. Lindsey's term as regent of the Ladies' Hermitage Association. They were brought to completion during the administration of her successor, Mrs. Reau E. Folk, with the full coöperation of Mrs. Lindsey and other members of the board of directors. Plans for the present edition were begun under the regency of Mrs. George F. Blackie and are being completed under the regency of Mrs. Robert F. Jackson. The purpose of this little book is to provide a small, easily readable volume on the Hermitage of Andrew Jackson's day and to bring out certain interesting unpublished material relating to this period. These additional notes, given in the briefest possible space, represent material too voluminous to publish at the present time, but too important to pass without some mention.)

Preservation and Refurnishing of the Hermitage.—The reader is naturally interested in the period which intervened between the death of Andrew Jackson and the opening of his home as a patriotic shrine, the authenticity of the relics, the degree to which the garden and the grounds are faithful to their past, and other details of the preservation of the historic Hermitage estate.

The Hermitage and five hundred acres of adjoining land were purchased by the State of Tennessee from Andrew Jackson, Jr., in 1856. At this time Andrew Johnson, another Tennessean who was to ascend to the Presidency of the United States, was governor. The original purpose was to tender the property to the United States Government for the establishment of a military academy similar to West Point, and such an offer was made to Congress by the State of Tennessee. The plan was not consummated, however, for clouds which gave warning of the great storm of internal strife which was about to break, obscured all other interests. The Civil War soon followed and five young men from the Hermitage—sons of Sarah York and Andrew Jackson, Jr., and of Mrs. Jackson's widowed sister, Mrs. Adams—went to join the Confederate Army. Only one, Colonel Andrew Jackson, III, returned.

Andrew Jackson, Jr., died in 1865, but his widow continued, at the invitation of the State of Tennessee, to live at the Hermitage until her death in 1888. In the following year, 1889, the Ladies' Hermitage Association was organized, and on April 5, 1889, the mansion, tomb, and adjoining buildings were conveyed to the trustees of the Ladies' Hermitage Association. After this first step the Association busied itself with the raising of funds for the purchase of furniture, relics, and valuable papers which belonged in the mansion and which Col. Andrew Jackson, III, had inherited from his mother. The major portion of the present collection was completed by 1900, and in that year Col. Jackson and his sister, Mrs. Rachel Jackson Lawrence, signed a statement which forever establishes the authenticity of the relics. Col. Jackson died in 1906, but Mrs. Lawrence lived until 1923 and under her guidance, as well as that of "Uncle Alfred," the slave who was General Jackson's body servant, the furniture was rearranged as it was when the old warrior lived in the Hermitage.

This work was not done without continuous, untiring, and devoted effort on the part of the leading spirits of the Ladies' Hermitage Association. Their work received national recognition in 1907, when President Theodore Roosevelt, impressed by his visit to the Hermitage, sponsored an act of Congress which provided $5,000 for additional work in repairing and preserving the Hermitage as a national shrine.

Library, or Office.—Among the most interesting of the unpublished collections of Jackson material is that owned by The Ladies' Hermitage Association. It has been the privilege of the writer to make a detailed study of this material. The library, or office, as it was generally called, contains over four hundred volumes. One of the most striking features of this collection is that such a large portion of it is the work of Jackson's contemporaries—not only in military and political subjects, but in biography, fiction, and poetry.

There are a number of Sir Walter Scott's works, including his *Life of Napoleon*, *Tales of My Landlord*, and others. There is Henry Fielding's *History of Tom Jones*, some volumes of Addison's *Spectator*, Dickens' *Oliver Twist*, Bunyan's *Pilgrim's Progress*, Jane Porter's *Scottish Chiefs* and *Thaddeus of Warsaw*, Milton, Shakespeare, and a score of others reflecting lively and varied taste.

The collection shows that it was acquired naturally and gradually, for the purpose of meeting the needs and the interests of the household. There are law books, religious writings, biography, technical books on military subjects, numbers of bound political pamphlets, current magazines, and a few newspapers, as well as the previously mentioned fiction and poetry. There are also various publications on agriculture, cook books, music books, hymnals, and, most delightful of all for the human touch it gives, a baby book published in 1805!

This book, *A Treatise on the Diseases of Children, with Directions for the Management of Children from Birth*, was published in 1805 in London. It was written by Michael Underwood, M.D., of the Royal College of Physicians, Physician to Her Royal Highness the Princess of Wales.

It was, most likely, the most important book at the Hermitage in 1809, when Rachel and Andrew took into their hearts the infant nephew who became their adopted son and heir.

Slaves.—No history of the Hermitage is complete without at least a reference to the slaves who toiled in its fields, attended the thoroughbreds in its stables, or performed duties at "the big house" with well-bred courtesy and ease. Some few live by name, but most of them, like shadows in a brilliantly colored picture, have passed into a hazy, undefined background. Alfred sleeps in a marked grave in the garden, only a few feet from his beloved master. Across the fence, a few feet from the family burying ground, are other unidentified graves—among them, it is said, is that of Gracie, Alfred's wife.

Andrew Jackson, during the bitter campaign of 1828, was accused of being a negro trader. Nothing could be more absurd to people who understand the conditions under which he lived. He bought slaves and, occasionally, sold them—but slave dealing implies constant trade in negroes for profit and the records do not indicate, at any period of his life, that he deserves the opprobrious term of negro trader.

Among the slaves of the early period of the Jackson household were more than likely George and Moll, who were given to Rachel in 1791, as a part of the property which she inherited in the settlement of her father's estate. Davidson County court records show that in the same year Andrew Jackson bought a man named Peter and a six-year-old boy, named Aron. In 1793 he bought a negro girl named Peg, about twenty-six years old; a little later a negro girl named Rock, aged about twelve years; and on July 8, 1794, "A negro wench by the name of Hannah and her child called Bett," for 80 pounds Virginia currency. Hannah rose to an important position in the household. She was, in more ways than one, to be Mrs. Jackson's right hand—she supervised the poultry, the household, and seemed to be, in addition to these duties, personal maid to her mistress. It was she who nursed Rachel in her last illness.

Hannah passed to Sarah York Jackson, by gift of General Jackson, along with Alfred, Gracie, George Washington, Mary, Augustus, Sarah, and others. (Slave deed—original at Tennessee State Library—dated August 16, 1854—A. Jackson, Jr.)

When the Hermitage was transferred to the custody of the Ladies' Hermitage Association "Uncle Alfred," by legislative request, went with it.

Senate Joint Resolution, No. 14, adopted April 3, 1889, reads:

> "Be it resolved by the General Assembly of the State of Tennessee, That —— Jackson, colored, an old manservant of General Andrew Jackson, who now lives in a small cabin within one hundred yards of the tomb of General Jackson, that in transferring the Hermitage to the Confederate Home Association and the Ladies' Association, by recent legislation, that we request the Trustees of the Confederate Home Association and the Ladies' Association, not to disturb this old and good negro, but allow him to live in his cabin until he is called to meet his master on the other side of the river, and rest with him under the shade of the trees.
>
> "Benj. J. Lea, Speaker of the Senate; W. L. Clapp, Speaker of the House of Representatives. Approved April 6, 1889. Robert L. Taylor, Governor."

"Uncle" Alfred, who was born in 1803, died September 4, 1901. In fulfilment of his dearest wish he was buried near the tomb of his master, where he does, indeed, in the words of the dying Confederate general, Stonewall Jackson, "rest under the shade of the trees."

Sword Presented to Andrew Jackson by Citizens of Philadelphia.—(Niles Register—Vol. 47—p. 402. Issue of February 7, 1835.)

> Philadelphia, January 1st, 1835.
>
> To gen. Andrew Jackson, president of the United States.
>
> Sir: The undersigned citizens of Philadelphia, beg leave, on the anniversary of the glorious battle of New Orleans, to offer, by the attention of their friend, Col. A. L. Rumfort, the accompanying sword, from the manufacture of their fellow

citizen, Mr. F. W. Widmann, as a testimonial of their love and gratitude towards the benefactor of their country.

The artist has endeavored, in the ornamental work, to depict that conflict, which resulted in the most decisive and glorious victory known to our American annals. Art may indeed be inadequate to do justice to such a subject, but its details will be indelibly engraved on the minds and memories of the present and of each succeeding generation of Americans, worthy of the name. In an equal degree must their grateful hearts be impressed with the image of the devoted patriot chief, who, battling for THE PEOPLE AND THE PEOPLE'S RIGHTS, is ever invincible, by foreign or domestic foes, by force or fraud, unconquered and unconquerable.

With sentiments of the highest esteem, we remain your friends and fellow citizens.

(Here follow the names of between 60 and 70 gentlemen.)

Washington, January 8, 1835.

Sir: I receive, with emotions of the deepest gratitude, the sword you are pleased to present me as a testimonial of the regard which a portion of my friends, in Philadelphia, entertain of my services at New Orleans, this day twenty years ago. In memory of the troops that coöperated with me on that occasion, and to whose patriotism and courage more than to the skill of their commanding general, the country is indebted for the signal repulse of the enemy on the 8th of January, I accept it with a pleasure which I cannot express.

I pray to you, sir, to convey to the gentlemen who have united with you in the presentation of this sword, my sincere thanks for the honor due me personally, and the assurances that it shall be preserved as a memento, valuable as a specimen of manufacture, and useful to those who will come after us, as a proof that the public service of the soldier will always find in the approbation of a free people the fullest reward.

Allow me, sir, to tender to you personally my acknowledgments for the eloquent and complimentary terms you have employed in the execution of the trust assigned to you on this occasion. I am, very respectfully, your obedient servant,

ANDREW JACKSON.

Col. A. L. Rumfort.

The Artist, Ralph E. W. Earl, "Court Painter."—Most of the portraits in the Hermitage collection are the work of Ralph Eleazar Whitesides Earl, who was born in New York City about 1788. He was a son of the eminent American artist, Ralph Earl, and his second wife, Anne Whitesides. Little is known of his early life, but information supplied the author in 1936 by Ralph E. W. Prime, Jr., of Yonkers and New York City, New York, indicates that he went abroad prior to the War of 1812, painted numerous portraits in England and France, and returned to the United States some time between the summer of 1815 and the early part of 1817. His long residence in the Hermitage household and his numerous portraits of General Jackson's kinsmen and friends caused him to be dubbed "The Court Painter." The correct spelling of the branch of the family to which he belongs is "Earl," although historians frequently add a final "e" to his name.

The Garden.—It seems appropriate to add to that which has already been written about the garden an important letter written to the late Miss Louise Grundy Lindsley, charter member, former regent, and member of the board of directors, of the Ladies' Hermitage Association, by Mrs. Rachel Jackson Lawrence, about a year before the latter's death. The letter states:

> "As you enter the garden gate, you find the fringe tree planted by Grand-pa. Passing down the walk, you find the crepe myrtle on either side. Along the border farther down, are lilac and syringa. At the far side of the middle plot, there is a smoke tree, and following the path down, you find lilac, crepe myrtle, mock orange, and along the back fence of the garden these same shrubs.

> "As you enter the gate on the left-hand side, is the calicanthus or Sweet Betsy. There are the fig bushes, the flowering almond, and many other shrubs. Around the tomb are the magnolias.

> "In the garden, the flowers were the June lily, lily-of-the-valley, single white and blue hyacinth, the red, the white and the pink peonies, blooming in succession as named.

> "The center beds were filled with the old fashioned sweet-williams, petunias, periwinkles, blue-bells, pinks, and other garden flowers. There were iris and jonquils, and, as we called them, golden candle-sticks. There was the coral honeysuckle,

which hung in great clusters, on the right side of the formal plot. Among the roses, there was the old-fashioned little yellow rose, the hundred leaf pink rose, the moss rose, and the large white cabbage rose. There was the Japanese magnolia planted near the center, the rare cucumber magnolia, the very rare tree peony. Like all old gardens, in the corners were violets and blue bottles. Box trees marked the corners of the walks. There were several evergreens around the tomb and a bunch of hickory trees planted by Grand-pa. Now this is all that I can remember. Signed—Rachel Jackson Lawrence."

Sarah York Jackson, who spoke often of the Hermitage garden in letters to her sons, wrote Andrew Jackson, III, in the spring of 1852:

"... all our early flowers are destroyed, also all the first plants of vegetables. You would be grieved to see our garden. We are making some few improvements in it this season, bricking around the beds, and have had a supply of fine roses. We have now about fifty varieties of roses, some very fine...."

To this gracious, devoted woman was given the privilege of guarding Andrew Jackson's Hermitage and its cherished garden through long, weary years of war, sorrow, poverty and neglect, until the hands of other women reached out to carry the responsibilities which Death alone caused her to relinquish.

FOOTNOTES

[1]The origin of the name of Jackson's Hermitage estate is obscure. Thomas Hart Benton, in his *Thirty Years' View*, Vol. I, page 736, says: "He ... lived on a superb estate of some thousand acres, twelve miles from Nashville, then hardly known by its subsequent famous name of the Hermitage—name chosen for its perfect accord with his feelings; for he had then actually withdrawn from the stage of public life...."

Mr. W. E. Beard, of Nashville, a well-known writer and historian, suggests that Jackson may have been influenced by the name of Aaron Burr's home. "Before Jackson's Hermitage there were at least two other homes, associated with noteworthy figures in American history, bearing the name. One was the Hermitage of Gen. Arthur St. Clair ... located near Youngstown, Pa. The other Hermitage was in New Jersey and has more romantic associations. It was the home during the Revolution of the beautiful Widow Prevost, the beloved of Col. Aaron Burr, later his wife and the mother of the gifted Theodosia.... One of Jackson's earliest visitors of note at his Hermitage was Col. Burr.... A reasonable supposition would be that the charming adventurer, remembering the days of his dashing courtship in Jersey, suggested the name for the new home of his host."

Mr. Beard remarks that Burr visited Jackson's Hermitage after its name was in use. In support of his theory it may be stated, however, that Jackson had known Burr since 1797. There is, as far as is known at present, nothing to prove definitely the origin of the name of Andrew Jackson's Hermitage.

[2]An old log building, said to have been Andrew Jackson's carriage house at Hunter's Hill, has been removed to the Hermitage.

[3]In 1817 Truxton, then seventeen years old, was presented by General Jackson to Col. Robert Butler, adjutant-general of the New Orleans campaign, who resided in the Mississippi Territory. "I drop you a hasty line to inform you of the safe

arrival of Truxton," wrote Col. Butler to General Jackson, on April 20, 1817. "I met him at Ft. Adams landing yesterday.... My dear Genl I feel under great obligations to you for this Horse of Horses. I certainly never beheld a more noble animal.... I shall cherish and pet him as a great favorite as long as he lives."

Military portrait of General Andrew Jackson done by the artist, Ralph E. W. Earl, who married one of Mrs. Jackson's nieces and was, for 20 years, a member of the Hermitage household. Earl was known during the Jackson administration as "Portrait Painter to the King." THE HERMITAGE, home of General Andrew Jackson, Seventh President of the United States, Nashville, Tennessee.

Portrait of Andrew Jackson on Sam Patch, white horse presented him by the citizens of Pennsylvania in 1833. Portrait by Earl. THE HERMITAGE, home of General Andrew Jackson, Seventh President of the United States, Nashville, Tennessee.

Portrait of RACHEL DONELSON JACKSON
—by Earl
THE HERMITAGE
Home of General Andrew Jackson
Seventh President of the United States
Nashville, Tennessee

THE HERMITAGE—Home of General Andrew Jackson, Seventh President of the United States, Hermitage, Tennessee, near Nashville. Standing today just as it stood when he left it over 100 years ago is the classic home of "Old Hickory." Built in 1819, this historic shrine has successfully defied time and nature for 134 years. Although it was damaged by fire in 1834, it was restored immediately as it stands today.

www.ingramcontent.com/pod-product-compliance
Ingram Content Group UK Ltd.
Pitfield, Milton Keynes, MK11 3LW, UK
UKHW040820280325
456847UK00003B/567